Dedicated to the thousands of people who have shared
their exceptional experiences with us over the years, and
to those who will share in the future. You are among the
greatest of teachers.

Dedicated to near-death experience researchers, past and
future.

Dedicated to Jody Long, whose efforts made this book
possible.

Contents

Author's Note

Due to the overwhelming percentage of loving and warm experiences reported in near-death experiences (NDEs), I occasionally receive e-mails from people, often in a depression, wondering if they should try suicide in order to induce one. I immediately respond: "Absolutely not!" I encourage those who are depressed to seek counseling and also to discuss their life issues with their health-care team. People who had near-death experiences as a result of suicide attempts almost uniformly later believe that their suicide attempts were serious mistakes. An NDE should *never* be sought by creating a life-threatening event.

CHAPTER 1

Introduction

We are in the position of a little child entering a huge
library filled with books in many different languages. The
child knows someone must have written those books. It
does not know how. The child dimly suspects a mysterious
order in the arrangement of the books but doesn't know
what it is. That, it seems to me, is the attitude of even the
most intelligent human being toward God.[1]

—**Albert Einstein**

It's easy to see why people are fascinated with near-death
experiences (NDEs). I have been intrigued by them for
many decades. As a trained medical doctor, I know what
should be possible when bodies break down near death.
At a time when no memory should be possible, when
people are either certifiably unconscious or even dead,
those reporting NDEs consistently describe highly lucid

and organized experiences. Many report details of what is happening to and around their bodies from a perspective outside of their bodies, details that are later verified by other witnesses. That should not be possible if these reports were merely the result of traumatized brains. Something else is at work in these stories.

But not only do these tales seem medically impossible; they also give accounts of a mysterious world that humanity has always been curious about but has never had direct evidence of: the land of the afterlife, a place where some meet God, dead relatives, and other spiritual beings.

In my last book, *Evidence of the Afterlife*, I surveyed over thirteen hundred testimonies of NDEs and demonstrated both why medically and logically these could not be merely explained away and why I concluded they were credible memories of people's experiences. I also summarized the most common components of these experiences. In this follow-up book, I survey many more stories, but this time I want to focus on the remarkable world people discovered on the other side.

Our situation regarding NDEs is similar to the way humanity learned of exotic lands during the ancient era of exploration. After sailors returned from long voyages and wrote their accounts, scholars would survey multiple accounts from different voyagers, discern where they agreed or disagreed, and come up with the most likely descriptions of the geography, culture, rituals, and traditions of a particular exotic land. We are in a similar position today when it comes to the world of the afterlife.

Near-death experiences are surprisingly common. A Gallup poll found that about 5 percent of those surveyed had an NDE at some time during their lives. From this and other surveys, we believe that millions of people around the world have had near-death experiences.[2] In recent times those numbers have increased, largely because resuscitation techniques have greatly improved.[3] People who previously would have died are now being saved due to advances in medical equipment and better training for emergency personnel. These life-saving measures would be expected to result in a higher incidence of NDEs than ever before.

Remarkably, the content of near-death experiences is strikingly consistent. Even after rigorously studying NDEs for over fifteen years, I still marvel at how amazingly similar these experiences are regardless of the experiencers' age, cultural beliefs, education, or geographical location.

By comparing these accounts, we begin to see a coherent picture of this other world. For example, one striking aspect of these accounts, which we will explore more fully later in this book, is the consistency with which a divine is described. Those who report meeting a divine being generally portray God as someone who radiates incredible love, light, grace, and acceptance. This is not religious dogma or theology, but one of the most consistent claims of multiple individuals who have encountered a heavenly being. In other words, people are not merely stating or projecting their religious yearnings or beliefs, but, like the explorers of old, are describing an entity they have encountered. The fact that they describe these encounters so similarly gives us confidence that they have, indeed, met the same Being.

My goal in this book is nothing less than to provide the most scientifically rigorous account of the afterlife world described by those who have had a near-death experience.

ENCOUNTERS WITH THE AFTERLIFE

Before we explore more fully the world of the afterlife, let me summarize what we know about near-death experiences in general. As I wrote in my first book, *Evidence of the Afterlife*, I first encountered the idea of NDEs during my medical residency at the University of Iowa as I was reading an article in the *Journal of the American Medical Association*. There Dr. Michael Sabom, a Georgia cardiologist, described how he had closely examined 107 case studies of people who had nearly died. Many reported that they had had NDEs and described their experiences in vivid visual detail. Dr. Sabom defended his findings against those who wanted to explain them away as a "fantasy of death" or as "manifestations of a hypoxic brain attempting to deal with 'the anxieties provoked by medical procedures and talk.'"[4]

This led me to read Dr. Raymond Moody's classic, *Life After Life*, the book that introduced the phenomenon of near-death experiences to the world.[5] A masterpiece of philosophy and logic, the book is now required reading for anyone interested in the field of NDE studies.

I continued my studies in radiation oncology, which is the medical use of radiation to treat cancer and which is still the specialty I work in today. But over the next several years after this initiation into NDEs, I continued to read about them. I was fascinated by the mystery of how people whose hearts had stopped were having conscious experiences that they often later considered to be the most profound of their life. "With blood circulation stopped, shouldn't lucid and prolonged consciousness be impossible?" I asked myself. Yet NDE accounts vividly described how consciousness left the body. "What is going on?" I wondered.

As I read further about NDEs, I became more intrigued, especially when I kept encountering both logic and evidence that made it hard to dismiss these stories. Like anyone else I wondered, "What happens to us when we die?" NDE case studies seemed to directly answer that question. In many areas of life, when facing the unknown, we often seek out those who have already experienced what we are facing in order to get guidance and answers. So if we are curious about what happens when we die, it makes perfect sense to listen to those who *actually* nearly died or even experienced clinical death.

As intrigued as the NDE case studies left me, at

this earlier time in my life there was little or no time to conduct more extensive research or to search efficiently for new case studies. For NDE studies to fully blossom, at least to my way of thinking, researchers needed hundreds of case studies from which to draw conclusions. To find NDE case studies in those days—this was in the 1980s—researchers often had to rely on word of mouth or referrals.

Then came the Internet. Before long this technology would connect people and make the world as small as a village. I realized that I could use computer technology and the Internet to reach out to as many near-death experiencers (NDErs) as I could. I figured I could get enough cases for a good scientific study. I devised a plan to do it, and even settled on a name, "Near Death Experience Research Foundation."

I have the greatest appreciation and respect for those who survive a close brush with death and have the courage to share their deeply personal stories. It is only when these individuals find the courage to speak up do we even have the possibility for a scholarly investigation of NDEs. I wanted to provide a safe and easy place where people could share their stories.

To formally investigate NDEs I established the Near Death Experience Research Foundation (NDERF). In 1998, when we could avail ourselves of the advantages of the Internet, I launched the NDERF website at www.nderf.org. The NDERF website has always contained a section where NDErs share a narrative and complete a detailed questionnaire regarding their experience. And I mean a *very* detailed questionnaire. The NDERF questionnaire currently asks more than a hundred questions, gathering in-depth information necessary to reliably understand both the individual elements in an NDE and the entire NDE. The number of questions in the NDERF survey has taken NDE research to an entirely new level, one in which we are able to discover more details and deeper meanings than ever before.

For instance, the NDERF questionnaire explores not only the NDE narrative but also changes that may have taken place after the NDE, such as changes in relationships ("Have your relationships changed specifically as a result of your experience?"), religion ("Have your religious beliefs/spiritual practices changed specifically as a result of your experience?"), and values ("Did you have any changes in your values or beliefs after your experience occurred?"). We will see later that these are rich areas to explore.

Of course, God and related aspects of the NDE are treated in such questions as: "During your experience, did you encounter any specific information/awareness that God or a supreme being either does (or does not) exist?" "Did you seem to encounter a mystical being or presence or hear an unidentifiable voice?" "Did you see an unearthly light?" "Did you see deceased or religious spirits?" and "Did you encounter or become aware of any beings who previously lived on earth who are described by name in religions (for example, Jesus, Muhammad, Buddha, etc.)?"

When the NDERF website was started in 1998, there was no way I could have known how successful this endeavor would be. NDERF caught on like wildfire and would forever change my life. Over the years NDERF has touched the lives of millions of people. Remarkably, over four thousand people have shared their near-death experiences with NDERF. With this many NDEs available for research, *what you are about to read is the largest scientific study of NDEs ever reported.*

All of this brings up another major purpose of NDERF. From its inception, NDERF has been a public service. A major goal of NDERF is to receive and share near-death experiences from all around the world. Remarkably, portions of the NDERF website, including the NDE questionnaire, have been translated by over four hundred multilingual volunteers into *over twenty different languages.* This would not have been possible without the amazing dedication of the NDERF webmaster, Jody Long. NDERF helped scores of people in the media find NDErs for television and radio shows as well as newspaper and magazine articles. Over the years, NDERF has received and answered thousands of e-mails. From the very beginning, all that NDERF does has been provided freely and without charge. NDERF is truly a labor of love.

The collective response from the four thousand NDE reports I have investigated in my career point to the reality of the world we call the afterlife. Unsurprisingly, almost all those who have near-death experiences believe that there is an afterlife, mostly based on their personal experience. Here are some common reflections found throughout the database:

+ Leaving my body confirmed to me that we can exist outside of the physical body.[6]

+ We definitely live on—eternally. There is *no* death. Simply a passing or a return to home.[7]

+ There was definitely an awareness that there is life after physical/earthly death.[8]

+ I was aware that I was somewhere that was magnificent and when I was surrounded with people I knew were dead—I was filled with love and felt loved.[9]

These comments reflect encounters with a world we want to explore more fully in this book.

AN OVERVIEW OF THE NEAR-DEATH EXPERIENCE

Before discussing my research findings, I'd first like to provide a detailed overview of what a near-death experience is and what happens during one.

There is no uniformly accepted definition of a near-death experience. For my research, I chose a common-sense and widely accepted approach to defining the near-death experience. As the term *near-death experience* suggests, there are two components: being *near death* and having an *experience* at that time. In my research, near-death experiences are considered to have happened only when individuals were truly physically *near death*. NDErs are literally at death's door. NDEs happen when persons are so physically compromised from an accident or illness that they are generally unconscious and may be clinically dead, with no heartbeat or breathing. During this time of unconsciousness, NDErs have the *experience* part of the NDE.

Throughout this book you will read about the results of several NDERF surveys. The largest survey included 1,122 sequentially shared NDEs—meaning they were not selected in any way other than the order in which the responders uploaded their answers to the questionnaire on the website. This larger study utilized the version of the NDERF questionnaire that immediately preceded the version currently being used.[10] The most current version of the NDERF survey includes many new questions relevant to investigating NDE content addressing God and the afterlife. The results from over four hundred sequentially shared NDEs responding to this most recent version of the NDERF survey will also be presented throughout this book.

These two most recent versions of the NDERF survey included the NDE Scale questions.[11] The NDE Scale asks sixteen questions about the content of the experience. It is the most validated research method available to help distinguish experiences that are NDEs from those that are not. A score of 7 or higher qualifies an experience as an NDE. The NDErs whose survey results we are presenting *all* had NDE Scale scores of 7 or above, further validating these experiences as definite NDEs.

Although no two near-death experiences are identical, it is remarkable that in thousands of reports there are consistent patterns of elements. This fact is part of what gives us confidence in their veracity. Our research, verified by many other researchers in this area, indicates that there are twelve common elements and that these usually occur in consistent order.[12] I describe these twelve elements more fully in my previous book, but will quickly run through them here:

1. An out-of-body experience (OBE)
2. Heightened senses
3. Intense and generally positive emotions or feelings
4. Passing into or through a tunnel
5. Encountering a mystical or brilliant light
6. Encountering deceased relatives/friends or mystical beings
7. A sense of alteration in time or space
8. A life review
9. Encountering otherworldly (heavenly) realms
10. Encountering or learning special knowledge
11. Encountering a boundary or barrier
12. A voluntary or involuntary return to the body

An NDE does not need to have all of the elements to qualify, but most do have several. Each of the twelve elements is a powerful experience, one that could be transformative in itself. Below are examples of each element from the case studies amassed on the NDERF website. Included also for each element is the percentage of NDErs who had that element from the NDERF surveys. NDEs quoted throughout this book are generally paraphrased for clarity. The original source of the quoted NDEs is on the NDERF website, which contains the original quote and entire associated NDE.

1. An Out-of-Body Experience (OBE)

I looked down at my son's incubator and wondered, "Am I dead?" But I was also thinking that it was okay if I were dead, because my son was all right. I was later given a photograph of him post-birth that looked exactly the same as what I saw, even though he was on the other side of the curtain.[13]

—NDE due to blood loss during a C-section delivery; contributor is a nurse

An out-of-body experience, which is the separation of consciousness from the physical body, is often the first element to occur during a near-death experience. The NDERF survey asked, "Did you experience a separation of your consciousness from your body?" Of

NDErs responding to the survey question, 74.9 percent said yes.

2. Heightened Senses

The colors were intense and detailed—patterns, textures, weavings of color and sound. I knew this wasn't of our world, but it was all natural and didn't need explanation. I understood the essence of creativity and could create my own visions: everything I thought became a vision and swirled around me. It was amazing! I knew I was being held in unlimited love, and that love was forever. It was like loving the way God loves, and when that happened, my heart opened and it felt like my soul touched the unseen creator. I knew God exists and that we are a part of everything.[14]

—NDE due to a car accident

It is remarkable that near-death experiencers, who are generally unconscious or clinically dead during their NDEs, usually report being *more* conscious during their NDEs than during their everyday life. The NDERF survey asked, "How did your highest level of consciousness and alertness during the experience compare to your normal everyday consciousness and alertness?" Of the NDErs surveyed, 74.4 percent indicated that they had "more consciousness and alertness than normal."

3. Intense and Generally Positive Emotions or Feelings

Never had I felt so good, no pain, and I seemed to be floating, as if I wasn't ill, with no pain.[15]

> —NDE from a reaction to chemotherapy to treat cancer

I remember going through a tunnel and sitting on God's lap. He was in an overstuffed chair and had his arm around me even though I was so small and He was huge. A blinding, bright white light shone behind Him. He was wearing a white robe and had white hair. He was talking to me, but His lips didn't move. He told me that I had to go back, it wasn't my time yet; there were things I still needed to do and experience. I didn't want to leave, but I didn't protest. I felt the most intense love that I've never felt before or since.[16]

> —NDE due to an antidepressant overdose in a suicide attempt at age fifteen

On the other side, the arms of my loved ones welcomed me home. The feelings weren't of this earth. The temperature was perfect—not too hot or too cold, like I was wrapped in a warm blanket. The intense love just can't be described in words.

Amazing peace and calmness engulfed me. Everyone who had passed before me, and some people I felt I knew from another life, all welcomed me home.

I felt content and safe, like I was in the care and love of God. And that love of God felt like the first time you see your baby or the first time you fall in love—multiplied by ten thousand.[17]

—Two NDEs as a result of cardiac arrest

Peace and *love* are among the most common words used by near-death experiencers to describe what they felt during their NDEs. The NDERF survey asked, "Did you have a feeling of peace or pleasantness?" When NDErs responded to this question, 77.7 percent selected "incredible peace or pleasantness." Another NDERF survey question asked, "Did you have a feeling of joy?" To this question, 54 percent answered "incredible joy."

4. Passing into or Through a Tunnel

All of a sudden I was inside a tunnel, dark and starry, like the night sky. There was a light at the end of the tunnel, but not white light; it was colorful, like all the colors of the rainbow. Something was pulling me to the light.[18]

—NDE due to a suicide attempt

The tunnels that near-death experiencers encounter are variably described. There may be beautiful colors in the tunnel or other beings present. NDErs often move through the tunnel at great speed, but essentially never describe a sense claustrophobia in the tunnel. The

NDERF survey asked, "Did you pass into or through a tunnel or enclosure?" To this question, 33.2 percent of NDErs answered yes.

5. Encountering a Mystical or Brilliant Light

I realized that the "I Am" was who I was and always had been and always would be. What bliss! I had a choice to rest in this truth and stay on the "other side," or I could continue to play the "game" of being an imaginary person. As I realized this, I mentally "turned around" and saw a light that was brighter than a million suns but didn't hurt my eyes. That light radiated all-encompassing and unconditional love and "felt" sentient—it had a presence—like it was God.[19]

—NDE due to complication of sleep apnea

I traveled through a dark tunnel toward a brilliant light, but it didn't hurt me to look at this light.[20]

—NDE due to electrocution

Although the mystical light in near-death experiences is often described as intensely brilliant, it almost never causes the NDEr discomfort to look at it. It is common for NDErs to dramatically express their attraction to and desire to join with the light. The NDERF survey asked, "Did you see a light?" In response, 64.8 percent said yes.

6. Encountering Deceased Relatives/Friends or Mystical Beings

I was having a baby, and the doctor couldn't stop the bleeding. I left my body and watched them working on me. Then a bright light was all around me, and the voice of my great aunt—who's been dead since I was a little girl—asked me whether I trusted my husband to raise my son. My aunt was telling me that my husband wouldn't be a good father and that he wouldn't be faithful. So I couldn't die. I'm legally blind without my glasses. I didn't have my glasses on in the delivery room, but I could see clearly what the doctor was doing.[21]

—NDE due to blood loss during delivery

There was this most amazing bright light. All of a sudden I was in the most beautiful place with the most amazing bright light. The sky was so blue. The weather was so perfect. I was outside on a huge open lawn. Every member of my family and all my friends who had died were there—even my dogs were there! I felt calmer than I've ever felt; I've never felt so peaceful or happy. Then my brother, who's deceased, came over and hugged me. He smiled and said it wasn't my time yet.[22]

—NDE due to respiratory arrest

When NDErs encounter deceased beings, they are

usually relatives rather than friends or acquaintances. NDErs may encounter someone during their experience who seems familiar, but they do not know who they are. Many NDErs may see a picture of a deceased relative later in life and recognize the person as the one encountered in their NDE. A number of NDErs describe meeting deceased pets. Whether the encounter is with a deceased person or pet, it is nearly always a joyous reunion. The deceased generally appear in picture-perfect health even if they died of a chronic or disfiguring illness. The NDERF survey asked, "Did you meet or see any other beings?" Of NDErs, 57.8 percent responded to this question by selecting yes.

7. A Sense of Alteration in Time or Space

No speed or slow or time! Only "being." I can see everything around me but don't feel any pain or stress. Everything is heightened and accelerated into pure light energy, with no sense of space or time. I'm more alive than I've ever felt before. No words can describe this transformation.[23]

—NDE due to motorcycle accident

I felt perfect infinite timelessness—I knew everything that had ever existed in the universe, and everything that ever will exist. Time is an illusion, just like our skin and bones and senses. Our carbon-based senses perceive carbon-based reality, but it's really a spectac-

ular illusion! My true nature was one with all. No time, just right now.[24]

—NDE due to overdose of anesthesia

Near-death experiencers commonly describe an altered sense of time during their NDEs. They often state that time as we understand it in our earthly lives did not exist during their NDE. The NDERF survey asked, "Did you have any sense of altered space or time?" To this question, 60.5 percent responded yes. Another NDERF survey question asked only about an altered sense of time with the question, "Did time seem to speed up?" To that question, 33 percent of NDErs answered, "Everything seemed to be happening all at once."

8. A Life Review

I watched from above and saw my life passing before my eyes. I had never heard about this before, but I saw every moment of my life like I was watching a movie. I was so young, I didn't have to account for sins or learn lessons, but I saw my whole life in just a few seconds.[25]

—NDE due to drowning at age seven

I didn't care whether or not I was alive. Instead, I focused on watching an immense, clear TV screen that was in front of me. It showed images of everything that had ever happened in my life—my entire life in pictures. And with each picture, I reexperienced the

feelings that I had felt at the time it had happened.
And this was happening all at the same time! I could
see my life in picture form and feel the emotion or the
lesson all in unison. In daily life, you see a picture and
then you have a memory. But in this experience, I re-
ceived complete knowledge of all my life events in vivid
picture form and memory at the same moment![26]

—NDE due to severe blood loss after delivery

During a life review, the NDErs review all or some of
the events that occurred during their life. The NDERF
survey asked, "Did you experience a review of past events
in your life?" In response, 21.8 percent answered yes.

9. Encountering Otherworldly (Heavenly) Realms

I was floating through pink and purple clouds. I was
a baby, and my grandmother was carrying me over
her shoulder. Two teeny cherubs with wings followed
us, fluttering like hummingbirds. One was pink and
the other was purple. I was giggling as I tried to touch
them. Then the scenery changed to green valleys and
hills and I could hear children laughing. I wanted to
go there, but a voice said, "No! You're too young!"
Then the atmosphere changed to brilliant pastel blue
and two huge golden gates floated in midair before
me.[27]

—NDE in very early childhood due to illness

I passed into a place of light, with rolling hills, grass, flowers, and vibrant blue skies. The intensity, brilliance, and clarity of the colors amazed me. They seemed to be emitted from within each part of the landscape. The green grass glowed. It was so beautiful.[28]

—NDE due to a head injury

A heavenly, all-encompassing light was everywhere. My pain was gone, and my body felt free. I was filled with joy and contentment. I heard the most beautiful music and thought, "So this is what heavenly music sounds like." I became aware of the peace that passes all understanding. I never wanted to leave. I was in the presence of Jesus. I didn't see Him, but He was in the light and spoke to me telepathically. I felt the overflowing love of God.[29]

—NDE due to internal bleeding from an ectopic pregnancy

The unearthly or "heavenly" realms that NDErs encounter are usually beautiful beyond anything on earth. There may be buildings, other beings, and stunningly beautiful landscapes. NDErs may describe these realms as having gorgeous colors that do not exist on earth. They may hear music that is beautiful beyond anything possible on earth. The NDERF survey asked, "Did you see or visit any beautiful or otherwise distinctive locations, levels, or dimensions?" When NDErs responded,

42.1 percent answered yes. Another NDERF survey question asked a more general question: "Did you seem to enter some other, unearthly world?" For this question, 51 percent selected "clearly mystical or unearthly realm."

10. Encountering or Learning Special Knowledge

I became one with all existence, but I still knew that I was me. Everything was okay, everything was love; I knew that the purpose of human life is for experience and expansion. I was one with the doctor, the nurses, my mom, the medical equipment, the sound of the machine flatlining, and all the space in between. I could have raised the doctor's arm up, but I didn't have any desire to manipulate his free will. None.[30]

—NDE due to an overdose of anesthesia

My grandfather, who had been a doctor and died when I was seven, appeared, wearing a white coat. He told me where the three main infections were located inside of me. He used Latin terms, though I don't speak Latin, and included some other medical details. Then he disappeared. I reentered my body and repeated to the emergency surgeon and my husband what my grandfather had just told me. A few days after the successful surgery, the surgeon told me that my grandfather's directions had helped him find a third infection that had not been part of the origi-

nal diagnosis. It was exactly as my grandfather had described it, in a hidden part of my pelvis.[31]

—NDE from the Netherlands involving peritonitis following surgery

It is not unusual for NDErs to acquire knowledge during their NDEs that they could not possibly have known from their waking life. The special knowledge may be earthly or unearthly (some call this spiritual) knowledge. The NDERF survey asked, "Did you have a sense of knowing special knowledge, universal order, and/or purpose?" To this question, 57.6 percent of NDErs answered yes. Another survey question asked, "Did you suddenly seem to understand everything?" To this question, 30.7 percent of NDErs responded that they seemed to know everything "about the universe," and another 31.9 percent responded that they seemed to understand everything "about myself or others."

11. Encountering a Boundary or Barrier

At the top of this mountain was a beautiful city. I knew some of the people there, but couldn't make out the faces of others. I started walking up the mountain to get to the city, but a voice behind me said, "No, you can't go up yet; it's not your time." I argued with the voice because I felt that if I could get to that city, I would be at home. Although I was in a field where I felt complete love, joy, and peace all around me like a warm blanket—completely protected and loved—I still tried to convince the voice to let me go up to the city. I started to turn around to see who was talking to me, but the voice said I couldn't see his face just yet.[32]

> —NDE due to cardiac arrest as a
> complication of surgery

The path ended, and there was just a trickle of water in the mud. Everything got lighter, like dawn, and I saw my grandfather dressed in white coming toward me. When he reached me, it was sunny, and I saw some people and a church in the distance. I asked my grandfather if he had come for me, and he said, no, he was supposed to tell me that it wasn't my time yet, I was still needed, and my questions would be answered later. I wanted to go to the church, but each time I advanced, the water swelled. But I felt safe and calm and happy.[33]

> —NDE due to a medication overdose at age
> fifteen

A boundary or barrier may be encountered near the end of the near-death experience. The barrier is something that the NDEr cannot pass over or through. NDErs have described many different types of barriers in NDEs. For example, barriers may be a bridge on the path they are walking on, a creek or river, or a canyon. Beyond the barrier NDErs may describe an even brighter light or greater beauty than what is present on their side of the boundary.

The NDERF survey asked, "Did you reach a boundary or limiting physical structure?" In response, 31 percent of NDErs answered yes.

12. A Voluntary or Involuntary Return to the Body

A pinpoint of light appeared, and I was moving rapidly toward it. A being of light who radiated peace and joy and compassion picked up my soul— not my body. I didn't care where my body was. The being was dressed in white and kept getting brighter and brighter. It seemed we were going up; God was everywhere. We continued moving into the brightness above. The farther up we went, the brighter the being became until I couldn't see his face anymore. We arrived at a little garden with a white picket fence, but I couldn't get in there. I was told that I had to go back. I begged and pleaded, but I was sent back to my pain-filled body in a rush.[34]

—NDE due to a prolonged coma from illness

At the end of the near-death experience there may be either a voluntary or involuntary return to the physical body. The question most relevant to this NDE element came from an older version of the NDERF survey, which asked NDErs, "Were you involved in or aware of a decision regarding your return to the body?" To this question, 58.5 percent answered yes.

As new near-death experiences kept pouring into NDERF over the years, I realized that there are more than just these twelve elements in NDEs. There are many other common and not so common elements consistently seen in NDEs. As you read the NDE examples in this book you can see this for yourself.

MULTIPLE LINES OF EVIDENCE

After summarizing these twelve NDE elements in *Evidence of the Afterlife*, the rest of the book was dedicated to laying out nine lines of evidence for considering these stories both real and credible accounts.

For instance, medically speaking, near-death experiences should be impossible. NDEs generally occur when NDErs are so physically compromised that they are unconscious, comatose, or clinically dead. Considering NDEs from both a medical and logical perspective, it should be impossible for people who are unconscious to have highly lucid experiences that are clear and logically organized. However, lucid experiences do occur at this time, and the level of consciousness and alertness during near-death experiences is usually even greater than what people experience in everyday life.

Additionally, the elements in NDEs generally follow the same consistent and logical order in all age groups and around the world, which helps refute the possibility that NDEs have any relation to dreams, hallucinations, or cultural projections. Dreams often skip around and lack a logical flow. NDEs are almost always a consistent narrative.

Another reason to consider NDEs valid is the realism with which people describe their out-of-body experiences. OBEs are among the most common elements of near-death experiences; in them people see what is going on around their unconscious body. What NDErs see and hear of earthly events in the out-of-body state is almost always realistic. When the NDEr or others later seek to verify what was observed or heard during the NDE, the out-of-body observations are almost always confirmed as accurate, even if the observations included events very far from the physical body. This fact alone rules out the possibility that NDEs are related to any known brain functioning or sensory awareness. This also refutes the possibility that NDEs are unrealistic fragments of memory from the brain.

Another convincing factor is that many near-death experiences occur while the person is under general anesthesia, when conscious experience should be impossible. Some skeptics claim that NDEs may be the result of too little anesthesia, but this ignores the fact that some NDEs result from an anesthesia overdose. The content of NDEs that occur under general anesthesia is essentially indistinguishable from that of NDEs that did not occur under general anesthesia. Powerful anesthetic medications are being used, and yet people have the same usually heightened level of consciousness and alertness that is seen in all other NDEs. This is further strong evidence that NDEs are occurring completely independently from the functioning of the physical brain.

This is a description of one such event from Kristy C., who suffered cardiac arrest during gallbladder surgery and went on to have a profound NDE. Here is her description of events:

> I was standing over the doctor watching them work on me. I wasn't scared, but fascinated. They were working extremely fast, and I felt amused because I was no longer in pain.
>
> Then I was pulled backwards into a tunnel with a door that opened into a spectacular light. The light was brilliant, but it didn't hurt! I passed into it, and it glowed with warmth, love, understanding, and knowledge—the knowledge of everything. Everything made sense. Everything was vivid; the colors were brighter and deeper. Everything was tranquil and peaceful when I crossed into the light.
>
> Then I was in a lush meadow covered with flowers and trees. I felt a strong presence, and I also knew my family was with me. The presence had a deep voice that resonated to the core of my soul. I don't remember what the voice said, but the peacefulness and calmness magnified. I wanted to cross a small free-flowing stream, but I wasn't allowed to. I wanted to stay in the meadow; I didn't want to go back because I knew that the peace, warmth, and light wouldn't go back with me. I tried to walk toward the stream,

*but I was pulled down and back through the tunnel
door. I left the warm glow of the light and was filled
with an immense sadness as all of the knowledge
and peace left me, my senses dimmed, and my vision
became muddy compared with the brilliance of the
meadow.*[35]

These are only some of the examples and reasons
supporting the claim that it is difficult to explain away
the reality of people's reports of NDEs. If you would
like more on these "proofs," please see the earlier book. A
section of the NDERF website, www.nderf.org/godev-
idence, further explores the lines of evidence presented
in *Evidence of the Afterlife*. This NDERF website section
also provides further details about research methodology, updated research findings, a bibliography, frequently
asked questions, errata, and other topics related to the
material presented throughout this book.

In this book, we want to take the next step. In my
opinion, if we have good cause for believing these stories,
then the most fascinating result of all NDE research is
what these explorers can tell us about their encounters
with God.

CHAPTER 2

The God Study

I gave in and admitted that God was God.

—C. S. Lewis

During the press tour for *Evidence of the Afterlife*, I was interviewed on *The Today Show* by Meredith Vieira. I was joined by Mary Jo Rapini, a counselor who had had a remarkable NDE after an aneurysm, an abnormal bulge in an artery in her brain, nearly took her life. On the show Meredith invited Mary Jo to tell her story.

Symptoms resulting from Mary Jo's aneurysm started when she was working out at a gym. She was rushed to the hospital, where doctors put her in the intensive-care unit. Mary Jo's condition worsened, and she lost consciousness. She then had her near-death experience.

Mary Jo saw a light unlike any she had seen before, describing it as "luminescent." She said, "It grew, and I kept looking at it, and it grew large, and I went into it. I went into this tunnel and I came into this room that was just beautiful, and God held me. He called me by name and He said, 'Mary Jo, you can't stay.'"

Mary Jo said the news upset her. She begged to stay, but God would not relent. Even when she talked of being a good wife and mother and a professional who worked with cancer patients, God insisted she had to return to her earthly existence. Then Mary Jo described what God said to her:

"Let me ask you one thing. Have you ever loved another the way you've been loved here?"

"No, it's impossible. I'm human," she said.

At that point Mary Jo said God held her close and said, "You can do better." Mary Jo then returned to consciousness.[1]

Right then and there, during the nationally televised show, I found myself thinking about the times NDErs had described encountering God in the NDERF files. After the show, the idea of God in NDEs kept popping into my head. Logically, I knew that one person's description of an encounter with God was anecdotal. It was inspiring, but not strong evidence for the reality of God. However, I now recalled that *many* NDEs posted on NDERF described encountering God, but I had just not focused on this aspect of their experiences.

"Why is the concept of God in NDEs virtually unexplored?" I thought. "Many NDErs report that they have encountered God. What do they discover?"

IN SEARCH OF GOD

Inspired by Mary Jo Rapini's NDE, I started a new line of research on the presence of God in NDEs. I began poring over the near-death experiences posted on the NDERF website, and it didn't take long to find the ones that described encountering God. In fact, the third experience ever posted on NDERF contained a veteran's vivid story of his close brush with death in the Vietnam War when an antitank mine detonated directly below the vehicle he was riding in. During that experience he encountered God:

> God took over my reins, in the sense that "I" no longer existed—only He existed. I felt overwhelming bliss, love, and compassion. The True Home and the True Self of all things were miraculously revealed to me.
>
> Ever since then, I know that God is. It's no longer a matter of faith or belief for me, but one of knowing because I have seen Him as He is. And He is loving, compassionate, and forgiving—which I hadn't expected. It's like He picked me up in the palm of His hand, and I'll always be thankful to Him for that; in fact, tears of gratitude still come to my eyes thirty years later.[2]

As I revisited NDE testimonials, I was surprised at how often people described encounters with God. I realized that NDERF had received over *two hundred*

NDEs describing an awareness or encounter with God. Having such a large number of NDEs that describe meeting God allowed me to be more confident that such an investigation could reveal meaningful results. I began a groundbreaking inquiry, which I called "The God Study"; it would become by far the largest study of God in NDEs ever conducted.

The study would investigate encounters with God in near-death experiences. I began to categorize my research to better understand the ways God appeared to NDErs. I first organized the log of testimonials shared with NDERF sequentially, not selectively, so as to avoid bias. By exploring the NDEs in this way, I could not be accused of trying to mold my version of God. An important point is that no NDE was excluded from the God Study due to its content. This was to further minimize any bias in the investigation.

It was also important that the God Study be transparent. I wanted to be sure that any who wanted to could go to the NDERF website and read for themselves the hundreds of near-death experiences that describe encountering God.[3] My goal was to make it possible for any who were interested or skeptical to review the entire NDE account, including the complete details before, during, and after the NDE encounter with God. This is a unique and important strength of the God Study.

As a physician and scientist, I knew that I had to put aside my personal preexisting beliefs about God and publish what I found in the God Study, whatever those results might be. I did not know where this journey might take me, but my overriding motivation was to learn the truth about God in near-death experiences. This was not to be a study of beliefs or opinions about God that NDErs may have developed at other times during their lives. The God Study was to be about exploring the *evidence* gathered *directly* by NDErs who *encountered* God during their experiences.

I made a promise to myself to stay within my area of expertise. This meant simply that I would not rely on writings about God in sacred texts, most notably the Bible. I leave it to the biblical scholars and others to compare the God Study to sacred text. In fact, I strongly encourage such investigation.[4] Comparing beliefs about God found in various cultures throughout the world to the content of NDEs was not the point of this study. The God Study was to be an objective view of the powerful experiences with God that many people report when they are at death's door.

This book is presenting evidence for the reality of God and the afterlife from research that is new and pioneering. There are virtually no prior scholarly studies that explored what will be presented in this book. Consistent with this book's focus on presenting groundbreaking new research findings there will be relatively few references to prior scholarly NDE literature. It is beyond the scope of this book to review prior scholarly literature regarding NDE as was done in *Evidence of the Afterlife*.

I analyzed my research in two ways: by reviewing the responses to multiple-choice questions and by reviewing the narrative responses to open-ended questions. The first means of research allowed for statistical analysis that was helpful for arriving at an understanding of the similarities and differences between people's experiences. In the second research method, which reviewed narrative responses, examination of first-person accounts containing terms such as *God* and *G-d* proved invaluable to understand individuals' encounters with or awareness of God.

THE STATISTICAL FINDINGS

The God Study reviewed all of the experiences shared by responding to the NDERF questionnaire from November 11, 2011, to November 7, 2014. For this study, experiences were categorized as near-death experiences if there was a lucid experience that occurred during a time of severe physical compromise that met the definition of an NDE as discussed in the Introduction. Regardless of the NDE content or the personal beliefs of the researchers, every account was analyzed. Consequently, the findings of the God Study are not an artificial result arrived at by including only selected NDEs that "fit the pattern" and excluding NDEs that "don't fit the pattern." This was vital for the integrity of the God Study. For such an important study I wanted to be confident that the findings of the God Study would accurately reflect what *really happens* when NDErs encounter God. As you will see throughout the rest of this book, the God Study found remarkable consistency in the description of God in NDEs.

The near-death experiences that were eligible for inclusion in the God Study met all of the additional following criteria:

1. Had an NDE Scale score of 7 or higher (which meant they first met requirements for even qualifying as a near-death experience).

2. Were shared in English.

3. Described a single experience.

4. Were shared by the individual who personally had the experience.

There were 420 experiences shared in the most recent version of the NDERF survey that met all of the previously discussed criteria for near-death experiences. All the NDErs answered the NDERF survey question: "During your experience, did you encounter any specific information/awareness that God or a supreme being either does (or does not) exist?" We worded the question this way to encourage NDErs to respond affirmatively if they encountered a supreme being during their NDE that was either similar or different from their prior concepts of God. Here are the findings:

Yes	191	(45.5 percent)
Uncertain	62	(14.8)
No	167	(39.8)

Narrative responses revealed that essentially all NDErs who answered yes to this question stated that they encountered information or awareness that God or a supreme being *does exist*. Essentially none of the narrative responses to this question described an awareness that God or a supreme being does not exist.

When I first realized that over 40 percent of near-death experiencers were aware of the existence of God or a supreme being during their NDE, I was shocked. This was an extraordinary finding! No prior NDE study had asked so many NDErs directly about encountering God in their NDEs, and no other study had reported such high numbers of NDErs being aware of God. To put this statistic in context, the percentage of NDErs who were aware of God or a supreme being during their NDE is greater than the percentage of NDErs reporting a tunnel, encountering deceased loved ones, or a having a life review.[5] This new information tells us one element of NDEs happens more often than any of these other NDE elements: *awareness of the existence of God*.

Another thing that caught my eye about these responses was that only 14.8 percent answered "uncertain." This is a notably small percentage, given that when the NDErs encountered God in their NDEs, it was almost certainly unlike any awareness or encounter they had ever experienced before.

In addition to asking questionnaire responders if they encountered information about or awareness of God, the NDERF survey also asked this group about their beliefs in the existence of God just before they had their NDE and then again at the time they shared their experiences. This was important because it revealed how an NDE might have influenced a person's beliefs in God. NDErs typically had plenty of time for any changes in their belief in the existence of God to occur. In fact, the length of time from the occurrence of the NDE to the reporting of it to NDERF was an average of twenty-two years.[6] This length of time would give the NDErs plenty of opportunity to learn from their experiences.

To get at this issue, we asked near-death experiencers directly about their belief in God. The first question asks, "Before my experience I believed . . . ," and the second questions asks, "At the current time I believe . . ." For both questions NDErs picked the best response from these options:

+ God definitely exists.
+ God probably exists.
+ I was/am uncertain if God exists.
+ God probably does not exist.
+ God does not exist.
+ Unknown.

The 420 near-death experiencers responses were:

Before my experience I believed:

God definitely exists.	164	(39.0 percent)
God probably exists.	105	(25.0)
I was uncertain if God exists.	68	(16.2)
God probably does not exist.	23	(5.5)
God does not exist.	21	(5.0)
Unknown.	39	(9.3)

At the current time I believe:

God definitely exists.	305	(72.6 percent)
God probably exists.	39	(9.3)
I am uncertain if God exists.	24	(5.7)
God probably does not exist.	12	(2.9)
God does not exist.	12	(2.9)
Unknown.	28	(6.7)

It is remarkable how much near-death experiencers' belief in God increases after their NDE. Before their experience 39 percent of NDErs believed "God definitely exists." At the time they shared their NDEs with NDERF, an average of twenty-two years later, 72.6 percent of the NDErs believed "God definitely exists." To put this another way, there was an 86 percent increase in those who believe God definitely exists after their NDEs. I can't think of any specific life event other than an NDE that is associated with such an increased belief in God.

It is informative to look closer at the belief in God of near-death experiencers at the time they shared their experiences with NDERF. If you combine the NDErs who currently believe that "God definitely exists" with those who currently believe "God probably exists," you find that this is the belief of a whopping 81.9 percent of NDErs—compared to 64 percent for the combined group before the NDE.

This dramatic shift in belief of God is understandable. Many NDErs experienced something beyond their wildest imagination during their NDE, something they never could have thought possible before their life-threatening event. If people experience a gorgeous unearthly realm of overwhelming love and universal knowledge and a joyous reunion with their deceased loved ones, it is not surprising that this might help them understand that God was a part of it all.

The statistical results from the God Study are very revealing. Nearly two hundred near-death experiencers claim to have encountered information that God exists during their experience. But not only did large numbers of NDErs become aware of the existence of God; they were also generally confident that their awareness of God was real. In other words, they felt confident that they were experiencing something real.

The NDEs were shared an average of twenty-two years after the NDErs nearly died. They had plenty of time to reflect on their experience and consider its reality. It is notable that NDErs maintained for *decades* their conviction that they *really did* encounter information about the existence of God.

It is highly unlikely they could all be lying or tricked by a subjective experience, since their reports are so similar. Can all of these people be wrong? For the evidence of the reality of God in the God Study to be dismissed, *each and every one* of the NDErs would have to be mistaken that they were aware of God during their NDE.

THE NARRATIVE FINDINGS

The statistical portion of the study found that awareness of God in near-death experiences is common and provides significant evidence for the existence of God. However, there is no substitute for reading NDEs; thus the God Study also evaluated the narrative content about these encounters with God. I carefully reviewed 277 near-death experiences that described meeting God and looked for the most commonly occurring elements. Reviewing these testimonials has been a lesson in humility. I have written about the NDE in numerous scholarly articles and in a *New York Times* bestselling book, yet often I cannot find words to do justice to what NDErs describe when they encounter God.

When I worded the NDERF survey question about awareness of God, I intentionally asked if they encountered "any specific information/awareness that God or a supreme being either does (or does not) exist?" I added the "or does not" part of the question because skeptics might ask if a significant percentage of near-death experiencers encountered information that God *does not* exist. In reviewing the NDErs' narrative comments following this question, virtually all NDErs responded affirmatively to this question, indicating they encountered information during their NDE that God *does* exist. The aforementioned question gave NDErs the opportunity to share that they either did or did not encounter information that God exists. Their essentially unanimous response that they encountered information that God *does* exist should bolster the credibility of their accounts, since there are virtually no examples of counterevidence, which is statistically very telling.

The narratives revealed that NDErs were usually highly confident that it *really was* God in their NDE. One NDEr responded to the NDERF survey question about encountering God or a supreme being this way: *"That was simply an 'of course' up there. There was no question about it."*[7] Many other NDErs shared their certainty that they encountered God:

+ There is no doubt in my mind God was there.... I went from an uncertain belief in God to a certain belief.[8]

+ I was speaking with God, so that is my proof that God exists. And I know there is another level to this "life" we are living. I don't know how to explain it in words; I wish I could plug you in to my memories so you can see what I mean.[9]

+ The existence of God and Heaven was verified. It is real—the light and the presence. It was clearly God—everywhere and a part of everything. There were no limits on the power of God. I felt unconditional acceptance, forgiveness, and love.[10]

+ The light that I encountered felt supreme—unending, unconditional, immense love, a force that feels eternal, powerful and creative at the same time, which satisfies my definition of "God."[11]

+ He said to me "Do you know who I am?" And I knew he was God the moment I looked into his eyes. I said "yes," and even though I felt ashamed and so unworthy, I felt loved like no other.[12]

+ Since I never knew God in my previous life before the NDE or in any organized religion, all I can say is yes, I encountered God. He didn't speak to me personally, but I felt him and knew he was there. He encompassed me. That's the only way I can describe it. Only God can make you feel like that, and he let me feel like that, even though it was only for a moment. I have been a believer ever since I got this affirmation that God is real. Existence after death is real. Life is a school, or a trip, or boot camp that spirits sign up for to further their knowledge.[13]

Although most of us have not encountered God in an NDE, all of us can appreciate the straightforward way that NDErs describe such encounters. Their descriptions of encountering God are as matter-of-fact as their reports about the events that nearly killed them. The near-death experiencers in the God Study were generally unconscious or clinically dead when they encountered God. It should have been impossible for them to have a detailed conscious experience while unconscious. And yet they did, and their experiences included awareness of the reality of God.

These NDErs were doctors, scientists, professionals, and people from every walk of life who took their valuable time to share their experiences with the NDERF website. Virtually none of these NDErs wrote a book about their NDE or shared their experience with a large public audience. The bottom line is that these NDErs had no reason to confabulate or embellish what they shared. I am not aware that an awareness of God occurs anywhere nearly as often in other types of altered consciousness, such as dreams and hallucinations, as during NDEs.

Hundreds of near-death experiences have been shared with NDERF describing encounters with God. These NDEs often tell of seeing God. Other accounts describe hearing or being aware of the presence of God. My research shows that an encounter with God generally had a lifelong impact on people's lives. Here is what some people wrote about their beliefs in the existence of God after their near-death experience:

+ The only things that are worthwhile are those that reinforce one's connection to God. The things that humans pursue on earth are mostly pointless and meaningless.[14]

+ I have strong faith now and can see where God influences my life.[15]

+ My faith in God is many times stronger than before.[16]

+ I no longer fear death. I have a connection with God that is very personal and is forever. It's not limited to this earth. I see life and death differently. I miss people who die, but I'm thrilled that they are at peace and no longer suffering the limits of this life.[17]

+ It was more than an affirmation that God exists. It can't be explained in words. . . . Saying that it's "proof" downplays this experience.[18]

+ I realized that not only was I made in the image and likeness of God the Father, but that He lives in me at all times.[19]

+ After my experience, I felt greatly comforted. I knew that God loved me and was always with me. I know now that no matter what this life brings, it will all work out, because God has it all under control. I trust that He will make everything work out for the good of everyone.[20]

+ I believe in God now. I don't question whether there is a God. I'm not afraid of "death." I don't make people question their own faith anymore.[21]

+ I told my favorite niece the whole story first because when she was eight years old I told her that there was no God and she had to take care of herself. Now I needed her to know that I had been wrong. God gave me knowledge that changed the way I live this life.[22]

+ Part of my purpose for coming back is to help other people awaken to the simple truth: *we are love,* we are part of God and cannot ever be separated from God. We've made everything so complicated! It's *not possible* to be separate from God—because we are all part of God. God isn't an entity; it's a living force— and it's *love.*[23]

These excerpts from the narrative sections in the God Study are just a sampling of the illuminating things people revealed about their encounters with the divine. As the following chapters show, people encounter God in various ways. I categorize these glimpses of God in three ways: love, judgment and insight, and heavenly realms. Each of these different ways of encountering God is unique, yet their unifying similarities (that you can easily see) help validate that they really did encounter God.

CHAPTER 3

Encounters with Love

Beloved, let us love one another, for love is from God, and
whoever loves has been born of God and knows God.

1 John 4:7 (ESV)

In the narrative accounts of people's encounters with
God during an NDE, the most overwhelming feeling
and description of this being is one of love. God in
near-death experiences is often described as profoundly
loving. God's love may be described as enormous, unconditional, and totally accepting.

Theologians sometimes talk about the *omnibenev-
olence* of God, which means that his grace and charity
toward others is unlimited or infinite. When NDErs
share about encountering God, this term comes closest
to the reality they describe. Here is a sampling of what
NDErs had to say about God's love:

- I felt the presence of pure love. This is very hard to describe. Everything made sense: God exists, God is love, we are love, and love creates all that is. Everything is pure love, God is love, and everything exists because of this unconditional love. I was surrounded by pure love. First I was cold and in pain, but then I was warm and comforted. I just know that God exists and that God is pure love and that we are a part of that.[1]

- I know that love is all there is and that God loves *all* of His children deeply and equally. There are no stepchildren in the family of God. We are all divine.[2]

- God loves us all infinitely.[3]

- I felt God as an all-encompassing presence—complete, total, and unconditional love in its highest form! I was surrounded by God's unconditional love, which was so much greater than human love. I was given the knowledge that God is real and loves me unconditionally—He exists and is real, and He is love.[4]

- I came to realize that God is more loving and caring than I could ever imagine.[5]

- No human can ever love with the love I felt in that light. It is all-consuming, all-forgiving. Nothing matches it. It is like the day you looked into the eyes of your child for the first time magnified a million times. It's indescribable.[6]

- The entire encounter was about God, the ultimate power of God, and God's forgiveness. The message was, "Love is the greatest power in the universe."[7]

Love is clearly an important part of near-death experiences and very different from love as usually understood in our earthly lives.

As you will see from quotes throughout this book, this experience of deep love often carries within it an affirmation of unity or oneness between all people or even all things. It doesn't matter if people nearly died in an auto accident or drug overdose, giving birth, or attempting suicide, they often come back with the profound notion that love and unity are at the very core of life's meaning. Not only are they the elements that seem to change lives most deeply; they are the ones that may put us closest to God.

Given the substantial differences between views of what love is among people throughout history, around the world today, and in scholarly academic disciplines, you can already see that love in near-death experiences seems more consistent.

To find out more about the love that NDErs so frequently talk about, I asked them directly about the love they encountered in the most recent version of the NDERF survey: "During your experience, did you encounter any specific information/awareness regarding love?" Immediately following this question the survey asks, "If yes or uncertain, describe in as much detail as possible." What was revealed in response to this question turned out to be among the most important in the NDERF studies.

GOING DEEPER

Between November 11, 2011, and November 7, 2014, 420 near-death experiences were sequentially shared using the NDERF questionnaire. As in the God Study, in investigating the role of love in near-death experiences, it is especially important to use a representative research method, not one based on a selection process that would introduce bias. For example, suppose that instead of studying love in the NDEs shared with NDERF, I studied love solely in popular, bestselling books. Critics would argue that this study group is biased, pointing out that the dramatic, yet atypical portrayal of love in these popular books might be why they became bestselling books in the first place. Studying NDEs as presented in this chapter helps deal with this concern. No experiences shared on the NDERF questionnaire were excluded as being NDEs solely on the basis of their content, including their descriptions of encountering love.

Getting back to the survey question, "During your experience, did you encounter any specific information/awareness regarding love?" the responses were:

Yes	244	(58.1 percent)
Uncertain	40	(9.5)
No	136	(32.4)

Of the 420 surveyed, 272 (65 percent) provided a narrative response to the aforementioned question. Narrative responses were:

Yes	232	(85.3 percent)
Uncertain	37	(13.6)
No	3	(1.1)

In order to study the 272 narrative responses scientifically, they were examined with the intent of investigating patterns, consistency, and inconsistency, keeping in mind that these narratives were drawn almost fully from those who answered "yes" or "uncertain" to the question.

Still, I was struck by the remarkable consistency in the responses of the NDErs. This consistency could not be explained merely by the NDErs' preexisting cultural or religious beliefs, since they represented a wide spectrum of those from various faith traditions or no faith at all. Below are examples of what people wrote about their encounters with love in their NDE:

+ Love is the paramount element of reality.[8]
+ I knew that the being I met was composed of a substance I can only call "love," and that substance was a force or power, like electricity. Love is the only word I have, but it's not the right word here.[9]
+ I knew that love was the greatest force around us and that we are all love, and love is the only thing that is real, that hatred and pain and hurt and all the negative things are not really the way it is, that we just create these negative thoughts.[10]
+ Love was everywhere. It permeated the afterlife. It was incredible.[11]

- I was loved unconditionally despite my faults and fears.[12]

- This love was unique. I felt completely safe; nothing bad could happen. I was no longer in pain, and all my worries and fears were left behind with my body. Not many can get even the slightest idea of what this love is like.[13]

- Love is All That Is. The word "love" is only the closest word we have—it's not really accurate, but I can't do any better with our language.[14]

LOVE BEYOND WORDS

As you can see, many near-death experiencers can describe the love they encountered in their NDE. However, other NDErs have difficulty in explaining the powerful and unearthly love they experienced. It is a classic case of words failing the situation. Here are some other representative comments about how NDErs felt in the presence of God:

- These incredible emotions were centered in the solar plexus—the most incredible mixture of peace, joy, love, acceptance . . . so strong I still cry thinking about it—that overwhelming melting pot of pure positive emotion: love, joy, acceptance, kindness, gentleness.[15]

- I still can't explain it thoroughly. You just can't. The feeling of God is not meant to be put into words, nor could it ever be.[16]

+ I had the overwhelmingly creative and unifying emotional experience of the presence of God. This presence is what is "real," and everything else is such a minor field of this reality.[17]

Any analysis of the content and themes of narratives of near-death experiences runs the risk of missing the forest for the trees. Drilling down into specific themes can make us miss the larger context of how transformative these experiences really are. In that light I have included some longer narratives that showcase how life-changing these encounters with love can be.

LIFE-CHANGING ENCOUNTERS WITH LOVE

"A Cloud of Warm Love"

Thelma S. was camping with her children in California when she was attacked by an assailant in a bushy area of the campground. She had always warned her daughters to never go anywhere in the campground alone, and now that advice flashed through her mind as she was dragged into the bushes by a man she knew, beaten with brass knuckles, and left for dead.

As she lay near death, Thelma had an experience of love that changed her life. Still, she says, words don't do the experience justice, but they are all she can offer:

I have not found words to tell of it. "Light"? It was much bigger, profoundly more than just light. It was so vast! Shimmering, a cloud of warm love. Like I was in love with the whole world, and everyone loved me back! It was such a glorious feeling, I didn't want to return.

Our life is a gift; we make of it what we want. There is a "God," for lack of a better word, and it would have to be called love! Now I understand some of my father's Bible.

Something very nice and loving came back in me. I left all my negative feelings behind and returned a newer me. But it has taken many years for me to put my finger on when this change started. Everyone has seen it; some think I'm more Christian than before. But I would say that I'm less what my father taught me as a child and that a more boundless and loving belief has taken over.

In a written postscript to her experience, Thelma made an interesting observation on bringing back to earth the power of love that exists in the afterlife:

There aren't any words to say what I need to say! But if every person who's experienced an NDE could stand together in one place, we would have such a "power" or "force" of love that everything on this earthly plane would be moved by it somehow or feel it in some way! Surely, the amount of love, peace, and nurturing feelings I had could change our cold world.[18]

"Even Now I Cry When I Talk About It"

Another near-death experiencer found difficulty describing the love she felt on the other side. Kathy W. was in labor with her second child when a complication resulted in her having an NDE. As she wrote:

Even though I passed out, I could hear everything. I was pulled backward from somewhere near my navel and left my body. I tried to shout that I was being taken, but my body didn't respond.

Then I found myself in a dark world where I felt pain and heard a deafening noise like a hurricane. Initially, I was anxious, but then through the pain I had a moment of absolute clarity. It was like discovering the truth of who I was—my essence. I had no body, only consciousness, and I knew I would gladly stay in that place forever and bear anything if it meant the safety and life of my baby. At the moment I had that thought, I was pulled backward faster and faster.

The light began to grow behind me, and I crossed a body of black water like glass. When I reached the other side of the water, I began to see and hear everything in my life all at once. I was in a large tunnel with walls like clouds, and loving voices spoke to me and coached me. They asked why was I there—not why was I in the tunnel, but "what was the purpose of my existence."

All this time I was accelerating toward the light and unfolding like a flower, although I had no body.

As I unfolded I felt it—the Love, which was like nothing I have ever experienced before. Even now I cry when I talk about it. I feel like I'm going to overload from just the memory. I was enveloped by light and felt one with everything—all-seeing, all-knowing.

This experience gave new meaning to that saying, "God is Love." The love was like an energy that connected every molecule in the universe.

After I adjusted to being in the light, I was offered choices for what would happen next. My consciousness continued to expand, and I realized that if I let it continue, I would not be able to return from death. I don't know how to explain it, but I could hear that point approaching and knew I had to stop it.

Then I became aware that I was back in my body and being prepared for surgery. I came back with immediate future knowledge and told the doctor not to operate but to deliver the baby using forceps. I also knew that I was having a boy. The doctor agreed to try the forceps but was ready to operate. In the end I delivered a baby boy exactly as I told him.[19]

"Surrounded by Unconditional Love"

Bruce had a similar experience in which he encountered God's presence, but had trouble putting it into words. He and a friend were out for a night of fun. They stopped at several parties. Then close to midnight they went to another where *"the beer, pot, and alcohol were flowing freely."* Bruce got caught up in the revelry, which is where our adventure begins:

> I drank five or six bottles of beer, along with two to three shots of whiskey. Within five minutes I began to feel very thirsty; I stood up to search for any kind of liquid, and all of a sudden, I experienced an intense pain across my chest. The last thing I remember before I left my body was falling backward onto the floor.
>
> Somehow, I knew I'd had a heart attack, died, and left my body behind. I was traveling through a tunnel so fast that I had a sickening feeling. Before I could adjust, I found myself in an ornate, light-filled room with a throne high above me.
>
> I had the sickening feeling again, but it was different: I wanted desperately to hide from the presence of God, but there was no place to go. I watched a review of my entire life—all the joys, difficulties, and sorrows. I saw myself being kind and being unkind to other people. I witnessed being ignored and ignoring others. I saw a love that had not worked out, and how others had abused me.
>
> I didn't hear words; it was more like telepathic communication. I had no problem understanding it. God was not pleased by my life of alcohol and drugs. Then I was shown a place of intense horror. I wasn't seeing it with my eyes, but in some other way. But then I was guided away from the horror by a kindly person I knew to be Christ Jesus.

I was comforted and found myself in the presence of many familiar people. I was surrounded by unconditional love and felt like I was "home." Then I was told to return to my life and was assured that everything would work out. I resisted leaving, but those around me gently urged me to return. I communicated that I needed to stay. Then these people I knew and loved urgently pleaded with me to return, approaching me one by one.

I could see that I was causing these people discomfort, and I knew I didn't want to harm them. They had come to see me, but I couldn't stay with them at this time. I knew that I would see and be with them all at a future time. I must return and complete a prepared task, or work, that will change others.

Just before entering the tunnel, I realized that everyone I had just seen had died, which shocked me.

Back in the tunnel, I traveled at a very great speed. My first sensation was of taking a deep breath. My chest expanded to its limit, and someone was about to pound on it with both fists. Everyone was talking at once; I heard, "We thought you had a heart attack." I barely had the strength to talk.

I now know that all humans are worthy of love, because each person has choices to make that have far reaching effects. Love is what survives beyond this life. I now understand that God is so much bigger than I had previously thought.[20]

Bruce's exposure to unconditional love took his life in a new direction. The past was no longer important to him, as he realized that many of his problems in life were related to his dwelling on them. Instead, he realized that the love he shows in the present is "the important part of life." After that he focused on passing on the love he had been exposed to during his NDE. It was then that his life took a more positive shape.

"This Will Heal You"

Michaele S. was driving home from the dentist when she crossed a railroad track and plowed into a passing train. She reached protectively for her nine-year-old daughter at the same time that she slammed face first into the steering wheel of her car.

Her daughter had only a few stitches, but Michaele literally bit the steering wheel, breaking off many of her teeth and leaving her brain deeply rattled by the impact. She stayed conscious long enough to see that her daughter was okay, and then she blacked out:

> *Suddenly I was outside of the car "standing" next to a being of light. The train was still hurtling by, but everything was silent. This being of light had the suggestion of a body and face and seemed masculine. It was beautiful. We didn't speak in sentences or with our voices. Whole thoughts were just conveyed—with complete understanding. I was "told" that I had a choice whether to live or to go on to the "next thing."*

Those are my words—the thought exchange is impossible to describe.

Then I was shown the essence of my life up to that point—not in little scenes rolling by, but as if my life was distilled. There was no judgment about my life—it just was. There was also no judgment about the choice I would make, one way or another. The "going on" was so enticing—I yearned for that. And then I looked down through the car windshield at my daughter sobbing, sitting on the car seat as far away from my body as she could get.

Looking at her, I saw this lifetime already in place with this other soul. There was nothing maternal in the choice I made, and again, there was no judgment. I decided to live this life, and at once the light being was taking me someplace. We were "moving" through a vastness—there's no other word for it—and at this point, language just doesn't work.

The vastness was, and wasn't, empty. We arrived at what the being said was Love. He waved his arm: "This is Love. It is always here, always streaming toward you, never diminishing, always loving you. All you have to do is open and receive it. This will heal you." (In that moment, I thought the being was talking about my body healing, and it was, but it was also about so much more—as I learned in the years following this experience.) I have never found a way to describe what I saw there; our language is too limited. Love was bound-

less, yet contained; no color, and all color; no thing and all things. It was tangible, dense, mysterious light. It was everything and nothing. It was a presence, but not a personality. It was all shape and no shape. I felt joyous in the most peaceful, quiet way, very grounded and accepting.

Then suddenly I was back in my body. I turned my face away from my terrified daughter and focused on my breathing. I could "see" my breath moving through my body. Then I was "told" not to swallow anymore blood, but to spit it out. I couldn't get out of the car, and after some time someone from the train raced up to the car and asked me if I was okay. I was laughing at that question, and don't remember what I answered.

Michaele had a *"continued heightened awareness and consciousness that lasted for several days,"* after the event, followed by a depression over the fact that she had to return to her earthly life.

I felt so changed, but none of the circumstances of my life had changed. I still had to deal with what I had created for myself before the accident. I had expected that amazing experience to magically transform my life, not just me. Thirty-six years later, I think it has. Love flows, and all we have to do is receive it. The intensity of that experience has never dimmed.[21]

"My True Essence Is the Energy of Love"

"All I remembered was the sensation of almost being pulled into a vacuum that seemed like a tunnel," wrote Teri R. about the auto accident that nearly took her life.

> *Lights were flying by me as if I were traveling, but it felt like a vacuum at the same time. Then I emerged from the tunnel into an indescribable place of peace and tranquility. The most beautiful Being of White Light was there. I knew that he took on an image so that I could relate to and feel comfortable with him, but his true essence was Light and Love.*

The Light Being Teri saw appeared as an older man with long gray hair and a beard. Beyond physical description though was the notion that "he loved [her] unconditionally." Teri goes on:

> *In his presence I felt like I was "home"—in a sense that I have never known before. I saw that my true essence is the energy of love, but as we reviewed my life together, I came to understand how I had removed myself from the benefits and bliss of love through anger. I saw how important it is to project feelings of love because other people can either benefit from or be negatively affected by my energy. I also came to understand that heaven isn't a place that you enter but a frequency that you attain. Being in the presence of White Light was "heaven." It was the*

greatest feeling I had ever experienced or dreamed was possible. Having that feeling again is what I strive for—not going to a place. The feeling, the energy I experienced became "the place."

I understood that you take yourself with you wherever you go. Your own consciousness has to change in order to experience the higher frequencies of love, peace, joy, bliss, and tranquility, which I felt a part of.

So I begged for the opportunity to do just that. I wanted to return because I knew that my consciousness didn't mesh with the unconditional love I was experiencing. I knew that I had to become more loving in order to experience this indescribable love permanently.

These are concepts that are difficult to explain, because they weren't conveyed to me in words. It was an understanding that spoke to me. But it was never conveyed as judgment or with the intention of creating fear. This White Light wasn't capable of anything but Love. With the insight I was given, I understood more about how things work, and I wanted to do better—not out of fear but because of love.

Teri recovered physically, but the feeling of love she felt during her NDE made her long to return to "where I had been during my death experience." Now, after working through feelings of anger from events in her childhood, Teri writes she has finally developed *"the ability to feel love for everyone, no matter what they do."* Teri writes:

> Now my goal is to feel nothing but unconditional love all the time. On many occasions, I still have to do some work to shift my frequency to love where I can feel the warmth of it in my heart, but I eventually get there.[22]

"My Joy Was Indescribable"

At the age of three, Katie was eating cashews when one went down her windpipe. She turned blue and passed out. Her grandfather, a fireman, tried unsuccessfully to resuscitate her, but was forced to declare her dead. During her NDE, Katie felt an overwhelming presence of love and joy that she could not make sense of until the next day. Here is Katie's near-death experience:

> When I died, I rose above my body and saw my grandfather trying to revive my body. But my body was of no interest to me, so I moved out of the room toward a presence I felt in the living room. I went toward this presence, which was in a brilliantly bright space—not a tunnel, but an area. The presence was one of peace, love, acceptance, calm, and joy. It enveloped me, and my joy was indescribable. I can still feel this spectacular feeling. I did not experience this presence as God (I was too young to understand the concept), but I did experience it as that which made

me. I knew without a doubt that I was a created being that owed its existence to this presence.

Katie recovered and awoke the next day. She went on to share:

The next day I knew two things for sure: (1) that there is life after death and (2) that I am a created being. I didn't know this rationally, but I expressed it by pestering my mother with questions: Who made me? What is eternity? What is God? She couldn't answer my questions but was wise enough to let me talk to others who could. I was so deeply moved by this experience that I've dedicated my life to the study of both philosophy and religion.[23]

"Embraced by an Overwhelming Sense of Love and Acceptance"

When she was fourteen, Demi went to the beach with a friend on the rough Oregon Coast. She was searching for seashells when she stepped into a deep sinkhole that took her underwater, trapping her in sand. What began as a terrifying incident, turned into a blessed event that has given her hope and understanding for decades. Here is her story:

I fought desperately to reach the surface, but the current was too strong. Soon I felt a sense of peace and love and was aware of my soul leaving my body through the top of my head. This didn't distress me, and I didn't feel sad for the body I was leaving behind; I didn't even look back at it.

Then I was embraced by an overwhelming sense of love and acceptance. I was in a tunnel surrounded with indescribable colors and music—unlike any colors and music I've seen or heard before. I didn't feel any fear—just an unbelievable sense of love.

Ahead of me was a light that was so bright I was afraid it would hurt my eyes, but it didn't. I knew that the light is where all things come from and where all things return, and that when I was back inside the light I would know and be everything.

I didn't see any people or sense their presence. I didn't see anything except for the beautiful colors, and I didn't hear anything other than the music. I was given messages—that is, I just knew them—and the closer I got to the light, the more eager I was to be in it, to "return" to all love and all knowledge.

The first message I was given was that the most important thing in the universe is love: love is all that matters; we are all the same, and we are all love. Then the message said that I was exactly the same as everything in the universe, specifically down to every single blade of grass. But, it wasn't my time to be there, and I had things I needed to do on this plane. This news upset me, because I had never felt such a loving and all-encompassing feeling, and I didn't want to lose it. I protested but was gently told that

I had to return to complete the things I was meant to do.

I had no sensation of returning to my body. My first memory was of being grabbed by my hair and pulled to the surface. I was angry because I didn't want to be back—I wanted to be in the light—and then I felt fear over what had just happened to me.

Demi says she didn't speak much about her experience over the years but continued to research its meaning and possibility. She went to college and took physics, biology, chemistry, and math specifically to understand how it could be that she was the same as a blade of grass. Upon learning differences between plant and human cells, she deemed the message impossible, since she could find no connection whatsoever.

Then one day she was flipping channels on TV when she came across a program about quantum physics, particularly string theory, that was an epiphany for her.

After years of searching for answers to that blade of grass message, I had found it. It was so clear—like being hit over the head with a baseball bat. Inside every quark, which is the smallest part of an atom, are millions of strings that are pure energy. They are different shapes and determine whether something is going to be a rock, an elephant, a person, or a blade of grass! That was my answer. I knew that we are all made up of energy; I understood the laws of physics.

> *I knew that quarks were divisible, and that they used the same verbiage: we are the same as every blade of grass.*[24]

Demi has had many challenges in her life related to childhood events, corporate jobs, and health, but she has "kept in touch" with her near-death experience throughout her trials and *"knows it's real."*

THE ROLE OF LOVE IN NDEs

I have included these detailed narratives as case studies in order to show the totality of how love and God work in these near-death experiences. As one can see, encountering "love" is often overwhelming and transformative. It serves much more than an affirmation of what many people already believe.

Let me summarize what we learned so far about the role of love in NDEs. We have discovered that a high percentage of people who have had an NDE have a profound and overwhelming experience of a loving being and/or of being fully loved. This love is often described by such words as *grace, acceptance,* and *forgiveness.* This reality is jarring and transformative for many people, often affecting the rest of their lives. Many say that this love is not only a feeling, but also a revelation of the nature of the world and even part of the very purpose for their lives. For many people this is the most important takeaway from their experience and what they return to again and again years later. What is most revealing is that these lessons and experiences are amazingly consistent among multiple NDEs.

But there is more to be found about love in these narratives, which we will turn to next.

CHAPTER 4

Universal Love

God loves each of us as if there were only one of us.

—St. Augustine

As we have already seen, people's experience of love in NDEs is often powerful, overwhelming, and hard to describe in words. But this love is also distinctive in its direction and focus.

The evidence from near-death experiences is that *God loves us all*. Again and again, one reads in NDE accounts how God loves us regardless of who we are, what we look like, how young or old we are, or what our shortcomings may be. We are loved by God for exactly who we are and what we are. For those who worry if God really loves them, this may be very reassuring. But it does run counter to the way even some religious people apply the ethic of love. The universality of God's love is a consistent and recurring theme in many NDEs.

GOD'S LOVE IS UNIVERSAL

"I Had a Connection with Everyone"

Wendy had abdominal pain for about a week. An ultrasound study showed such a serious abnormality that she was scheduled for emergency surgery. In her words: *"I had died during surgery from what I saw. I do not know how long, but long enough for them to perform CPR."* Here is her near-death experience:

> All of the sudden I floated out of my body. I felt free and peaceful, and I had no pain. I looked down and they were doing CPR on me. I continued to float up, and a beautiful tunnel appeared with a bright light at the end of it. The light was brighter than the sun, pure and white, but it didn't hurt my eyes.
>
> I knew that I had died and would be leaving behind my baby and my husband, but I didn't care. I wanted to go into the light. I wanted to go home. I felt like a blanket of love was wrapped around me. When I went through the light, all my dead relatives were there. I knew everyone even though I hadn't met them before. They were so happy to see me and welcomed me home. Even though they appeared in human form, I sensed that that wasn't their true

form. I had a connection with everyone—like some kind of collective consciousness.

I feel so many emotions recalling the experience, but nothing can really express those feelings. Everything was "pure"—the brightest colors—like a filter had been removed and I could see the purity of everything.

Then I turned and saw what I believe was God. It was pure energy, and you could sense the great wisdom that was within. God told me that we all have to live in love, that I had to take back the message of love.

Then I was in a meadow in the mountains and my grandmother was running toward me with children. She took me by the hand, and we stood on a bridge over a small creek and talked about my life since she had died (I was nine when she died of a brain tumor). She was so vibrant and healthy. I told her how much I missed her, and she said that she watches over me and my son.

Then she told me that I had to go back, that it wasn't my time yet. She said there is no time here, that time was made by humans. I understood what she meant. I wanted to stay, but she said it wasn't my time. All of the sudden I was falling back through the tunnel, the light was getting farther away from me, and then I felt excruciating pain because I was back in my body.

> *Love is the message that God told me to take
> back. We need to love one another and help one
> another. Meeting God and his speaking to me was
> that blanket of love. I use the male pronoun but there
> was no gender. The feeling of the love being wrapped
> around me, the brilliant colors, and the connection—
> now I try to spread God's message of love.*[1]

Wendy felt "connected to everyone" and came away
with a sense that her mission was to "spread the message
of love" God had given her. As we have already seen, this
is not a unique experience of those who have encountered God in an NDE.

"I Sensed God's Love for Me and for All"

Veronica is not sure if it was wasps or black hornets that
stung her multiple times, but she is sure that her allergic
reaction to these stings resulted in anaphylactic shock.
Here is her NDE:

> *I could hear the paramedics discussing how bad things
> were, and the last words I remember were, "We don't
> have a pulse; she's flatlining." Then I was gone.*
>
> *I went directly to a place of light—no tunnel or
> any sensation of travel. It was immediate, and calm. I
> perceived the place to be the exterior to an entryway,
> but not fully in heaven. There wasn't much light, but
> I could see vague outlines—of one major being of love
> and many other beings of love with souls.*

There was nothing but love, goodness, and truth,
with no room for fear or evil. Just all things that had
to do with love. It was beyond perfect and loving as
we know in our human state. No words can describe
it. I was so happy to be there.

I understood the major superior being of love to
be God, and I sensed God's love for me and for all.
That was the most emotionally intense and beautiful moment. There were other loving beings with
God—like his spiritually evolved helpers or com-
panions. God is perfect, heartbreakingly complete,
highly evolved love; yet He is a being with a soul and
identity. I sensed that we all are on a path to that
love and to God.

Our main purpose is love and realizing the source
of that love, which is God. Our purpose and goal is
God and His perfect love: to serve God, to love and
serve each other, to love ourselves, to grow spiritually.
We must understand God's love—and the opposite
of it and how destructive and wrong it is. Then we
must reach toward God to a beautiful and loving
existence.

No words can describe my time with God and
His perfect love. The type of love God exudes and
is all about is beyond human comprehension. God,
love, growing spiritually, serving in love, uniting in
love are our goals. Our lives are only approximations
of what we can achieve through God and His love.
Our love is immature and "seen through a glass

darkly." The answer is in God's light and love. The total bliss.[2]

I could go on with near-death experience accounts that show God's love. Veronica said it well: "When I sensed God's love for me and for all . . . probably that was the most emotionally intense and heartbreakingly beautiful moment." NDE accounts describe God's love as enormous and unconditional. NDErs consistently describe the love of God as profound and beyond anything that we could possibly experience on earth.

GOD AND LIGHT

According to these reports, God's love for each of us is complete, deep, and without reservation and extends to everyone and everything. It is probably worth imagining what would happen if this revelation were embraced worldwide.

When God is seen in near-death experiences, it is common for there to be an unearthly light present. We are all aware of light in our everyday lives, but the light of God goes beyond what is familiar to us.

"We Are All Pieces of the Same Light"

A good example of this comes from Andy. Andy's high-school graduation was to be in a few days. He went swimming in a cold lake, developed muscle cramps, and nearly drowned. "*Down I go again, deeper than before,*" wrote Andy in describing his NDE. "*My arms feel frozen in place, and every muscle in my body screams with pain. I never imagined that I could be in such unbearable pain. I sink deeper as the beautiful June sunlight fades to blackness. 'Oh my God, it's all black. I can't see anything.'*" As Andy was descending into a horrible darkness, he lost consciousness and reports encountering God's light:

> *I am instantly drawn toward the Light—I can feel its brightness, warmth, and love. As I get closer to it, I am absorbed by its brilliance and perfect love. Oh my God, I am the Light!*
>
> *I look into the Light's source and see a massive, human silhouette that is radiating with the brightness of thousands of suns. Even though I've never seen this form before, I recognize it and it speaks to me: "Andy, don't be afraid. Andy, I love you. Andy, we love you."*
>
> *The Light knows me, knows my name! Surrounding this Light form are millions of other Lights welcoming me back home. I know them all and they know me; we are all pieces of the same Light. I tell them, "It's good to be back home." I know we're all home together again.*
>
> *Although I'm in the Light and the Light is in me, I'm still Andy. I'm everywhere and here at the same time. I'm a person but also infinite, warm, and loving Light.*

I've never heard the Light's voice before, but it's not unfamiliar. And the Light has a beautiful smile that I also recognize. We talk and laugh together. The Light has the answers to all the questions in the universe—and I don't have any questions, because I know everything that the Light knows, which is to say, everything!

The Light also knows everything that I've ever done and will do but loves me unconditionally. The Light loves me because I'm Andy—a piece of the Light. There is no fear, no judgment, punishment, blame, or shame. No ledger of good and bad deeds. Only warmth, peace, joy, happiness, forgiveness, and love in the Light. I'm one with the unconditionally loving Light. I'm home forever.

And then I'm startled because the Light says, "Andy, you must go back." And I say, "No, I'm never going back." But the Light says again, "Andy, you must go back."[3]

This experience changed Andy's life. He now believes *"We are all One in the Light with God."* This is a point often made by NDErs: that God is not just for them alone, but for all of us. And somehow this truth may be associated with God's quality as light.

"Awed, Struck Dumb, Amazed, Overwhelmed"

Martin was fourteen years old and experimenting with dangerous drugs. He overdosed. Martin chillingly de-

scribes his heart beating erratically before it stopped. He
lost consciousness and had this near-death experience:

> *I had been floating or flying, but now I was standing
> on the "floor" of a "hall" looking toward the "far end"
> of it. God was there. Or more accurately, a great Fire
> or Light that I understood "represented" or "stood
> for" God. (But it was also really God. I can't explain
> this paradox; it was just something I had to accept.
> But that wasn't a problem because there was no "in-
> tellectualizing," just the raw, naked experience of the
> Presence of God.)*
>
> *I can't describe how I felt. I was awed, struck
> dumb, amazed, overwhelmed. But these words don't
> describe what a profound experience this was. God
> was totally "beyond" anything I had ever imagined—
> beyond language and thought, utterly beyond, but at
> the same time right there in front of me, mysteriously
> near and "accessible." This can seem so lame now:
> total love, total goodness, total knowing.*
>
> *And God "spoke" to me! Not with any words but
> directly to my mind. And what he "said" was so pro-
> found; I can't repeat it in words, but the gist of it was:
> "You don't really know yourself, do you?"*
>
> *God's question seemed simple but also had other
> meanings, like: "You don't know anything, do you?"
> And "Nobody knows anything, do they?" Meaning
> that we don't know how to love, how to exist, with
> the full and complete awareness and acceptance of*

*the fact that God is. What could I say? I had to
admit that, no, I didn't know anything. After all, I
was standing there right in front of God, who knows
everything! So I had to go back. God knew it, and
I knew it. End of discussion. I was disappointed. I
thought I would "go on" into the Light, but dutifully
and sadly I turned around to go back.*[4]

For Martin God could be described as either "light"
or "fire," although neither captured the full reality of
what he experienced.

"The Light Was like a Boundary"

Near-death experiencers use earthly words to describe
their unearthly encounters with God. Sometimes it
seems that all of the words in the dictionary cannot
adequately describe their remarkable experiences with
God. Such is the case with Lloyd, who had an NDE as
a result of a severe allergic reaction to medication. Lloyd
encountered the light of God:

*The light was like a boundary, but transparent. I
passed into the light. It's hard for me to find the
words to describe my feelings. I was blinded by the
light, unable to see anything, but the light didn't hurt
my eyes. It was like looking into the sun a million
times over, a pure white light. I felt warm, safe, and
peaceful and in the presence of pure, unconditional
love. The light was absorbing me, and my life was*

being shown to me. Maybe I cried. I was ashamed,
but I felt the love and knew everything was all right.
I know I was in the presence of God.[5]

Lloyd's near-death experience included an important message of reassurance: "*I also sensed or knew that a son whom I lost in an accident at the age of thirty-two was safe and in the light. I know now that death is not the end. There is life after death.*"

For Lloyd, God's light was a boundary marker, intense, pure, and linked to God's love. Again, these associations have all already shown up in earlier examples and are common references for descriptions of the unearthly light people encounter.

"I Was Made of the Same Light"

Anna had just given birth to her son when she started bleeding. "*The gush of blood . . . all of a sudden turned into an endless river,*" she wrote. She went into a coma and had a near-death experience:

> *The one word I'd use to describe the experience or journey would be "reality." It was the most real thing that's ever happened to me. The life I'd been living was an insignificant experiment that I'd volunteered for. The me, the I, wasn't Anna, the woman who'd just given birth. I was a light being—"light" in every sense. I was made of the same light as the light that shone from the clear pool in front of me. The light*

sensed and felt everything, thought and understood everything; it knew I was finally back home! And I sensed "light" as in lightness—no gravity, no strings attached. I was so happy that I wouldn't have to sleep or eat anymore, I would never feel tired again, no negativity, no anxieties. You just float lightly, dancing and singing with no audiovisuals. You're just being— that's what we're for—to be! The light was God.[6]

What is fascinating about Anna's account is her realization that she was *"made of the same light"* and that God was also the light. This shows how "light" captures the universality of what these people are experiencing.

God's Light

Here are more examples of how other near-death experiencers describe God and light:

+ The light penetrated me fully; I had never felt love like that before. Every cell in my body was full of love from the light, and I began to laugh and cry. I was crying for joy, because I knew I was delivered into God's light, and I laughed at myself for doubting I ever would be.[7]

+ At the end of the tunnel was the brightest white light that I've ever seen! When I looked at it, the light didn't hurt me like our sun would. I knew that when I touched that light, I would die. The light was God. I wasn't afraid of going there.[8]

* The light was God, and it infused everything.[9]

* The light was God—no doubt in my mind. It was total creation, and it was all around me. Every place I looked I could see the light.[10]

* I saw a bright light that was a thousand times brighter than the sun and felt that the rays shining down on me were made of peace, love, and serenity. I was safe, I was home, and I belonged. Yes *God* was the bright light I saw.[11]

* Even though I'm a writer, I can't find any words to explain the perfection I saw. It's like trying to explain a color that your eyes can't see. I knew that my soul was immortal and it is destined to return to where it came from. God was behind the light I saw, and I wanted to return to Him.[12]

GOD'S APPEARANCE

When near-death experiencers encounter God, it seems that the most common word used to describe God's appearance is "light." When NDErs further describe how God appeared to them, their descriptions of God may vary.

Lucia found this out for herself. She had a severe allergic reaction to medications given before surgery. Lucia says: *"The last thing I heard while I was in my body was the heart monitor give out a flat sound, like you hear on the movies when someone dies."* During her NDE she encountered God:

I was in front of this being, and I knew he was holy. I felt this was God appearing to me as I had always imagined him: an old man with a large beard. He had taken on this persona so that I wouldn't be afraid. I felt safe. I have never felt so safe in my life.[13]

The sentiment that God may choose different appearances in near-death experiences was repeated by another NDEr, who shared:

I believe that a person's experience is unique to their mind-set and belief system. I didn't need to see God or Jesus or a human figure because I have always understood there could be a God that was a "being" but not necessarily "human."[14]

Here are what other near-death experiencers have to say about God's appearance:

+ He was the most beautiful being I ever saw. I was enveloped in pure love and peace and well-being, a feeling I can't describe. I felt safe, a glowing love like no other. He was the big cheese. That's what I call him now. It was *God*, a supreme being, the one. He had long white, wavy hair past his shoulders. It was the color of that fiberglass stuff in furnace filters. It looked softer than anything I had ever seen. He also had a long, wavy, soft white beard that went down to the middle of his chest. His skin was golden bronze in color, almost like a metal. He was the

most beautiful thing I had ever seen. He was wearing
a kaftan with bell sleeves and gold embroidery around
the collar, sleeves, and hem. It was made of a thin,
silky, flowing rayon and had a Nehru collar. You could
tell he was buff under the kaftan. I was in pure love,
but it wasn't sexual. His eyes were a color that isn't in
our human rainbow. When I looked into his eyes, all
the secrets of the universe were revealed to me.[15]

+ Imagine a three-dimensional ball of intense energy
made up of golden white light. In the center of
the ball was the figure of a person—I couldn't tell
whether it was male or female. Around the ball were
smaller balls of energy traveling in different directions
and made up of all different colors that circled the
outside of the ball. But the form didn't and doesn't
matter. The point is the energy that the form gave
off. Once you have "experienced" that energy, form
doesn't matter. I knew who it was by recognizing and
knowing the energy the form gives off.[16]

+ I believed I saw God, not as a female as I thought,
but as a man. God was shaped more like an aurora
borealis crystalline mist in the shape of man.[17]

+ God is indescribable, unimaginable, and not
human.[18]

CONNECTEDNESS

Many NDEs also share messages about unity with God
or the universal presence of God. Bella's NDE included

an interesting future vision of her own grave if she chose not to return to her earthly life. "At age six, seven, or eight in a dream I was told I would have an opportunity to live or die before I was twenty-four years old. The water-skiing accident occurred three months and twelve days before my twenty-fourth birthday." During this accident, Bella encountered God:

> I felt "part of the whole" completeness; I was totally immersed in the totality of everything. I felt in the presence of God. I knew who I was, but I didn't feel pain and I wasn't afraid. I was surrounded by a tremendous white light and felt unbelievable peace, love, harmony, and goodness. I sensed goodness all around me; and then I sensed a question being asked—whether I was ready to die. I was conflicted. I saw my grave and my two children standing next to their dad, crying. I sensed I couldn't leave my children.
>
> My soul recognized an entity as God. I was part of a great white light, and I sensed many entities filled with love, goodness, peace. Words are hard to find to describe the Oneness-with-All state of being that I entered. Each soul is connected; each has a purpose, and each person is meant to perfect skills required to fulfill the purpose of that soul.[19]

About her NDE Bella added: "It was real. It did affect my life in very positive ways. It did teach me humility; it did confirm God's existence and the fact we are all part of one Whole."

ONENESS WITH GOD

The consistent description of connection and unity with God in near-death experiences surprised me. There was nothing in my prior religious studies that prepared me for this. But NDErs kept sharing their dramatic descriptions of our extraordinary oneness with God.

Puzzling over this, I had an "Aha" moment while reading the dictionary definition of *love*. The definition of love indicates that *attachment* is a defining characteristic of love. God in NDEs certainly seems attached to, even united with all of us. The very dictionary definition of *love* helped me to understand that God's exceptional love would manifest as an exceptional attachment, a unity and oneness expressing God's overwhelming love for us all.

Many other near-death experiencers shared about the unity and oneness with God they encountered in their NDEs:

+ I became aware that I am the light also. We are all part of the light. Each soul is part of the whole, or God.[20]

+ I didn't see God with eyes, but God was everything and everywhere. There was no separation felt.[21]

+ We are all brothers and sisters under the skin, and we all exist under the hood of one God.[22]

+ I was one with God or the Collective Soul, Father Sky, a Higher Power, whatever label you wish to attach to it. It was perfect love.[23]

+ I was aware of a oneness, a connection with God and all the other souls, but also individuality.[24]

+ We are all one. One is God. The separation of one into two is life.[25]

INTENSITY OF THE EXPERIENCE

In so many near-death experiences there is much passion and intensity in the encounter with God. You can see this in Michael's NDE. He was in undergoing surgery at age sixteen when his heart stopped. The moment his heart stopped, his NDE started:

> It was as if I had been immersed in some kind of essence or form of energy that I can only describe as the purest form of "love" that there is. It was wonderful—as if my soul had been blended with the soul of what we perceive to be God. There was no way to tell where I began and where I ended. I wasn't in a body; instead, I was in, around, and part of an immense, wondrous, overwhelming sensation of love and understanding. And I was completely at ease.
>
> I knew what had taken place from a physical standpoint, but I had no worries about any of the consequences of the end of my physical life. I was in a whole different place, and it was a much more wonderful place to be. I wanted to stay there. I felt utter peace, tranquility, bliss, and love—all at the same time! Words simply pale in comparison to the feeling

and can't describe how wonderful I felt to be there. Why would anyone not want to stay there? Now I feel like everyone will become one with God when their time comes.[26]

GOD'S OMNIPRESENCE

Many people ask "Where is God?" at some time in their lives. After studying near-death experiences, I believe they suggest that the answer is "God is everywhere." Theologians use the term *omnipresence* to describe this attribute of God. This is entirely consistent with the connection and unity of God with all that near-death experiencers often encounter in their NDEs. According to many of these reports, we have never been apart from God in our earthly lives and never will be.

The profound and reassuring message of NDErs is that God is with us every moment, in our earthly life and in the afterlife, and that God loves *everyone*.

CHAPTER 5

Purpose, Meaning, and Relationships

Accounts of near-death experiences are powerful to read. At their heart they are about people at the precipice of death who encounter a spiritual world filled with wisdom, understanding, and love. All of these elements have a power in their own right, but it's the power of love that stands out in so many of the case studies.

Sometimes, after a day of dealing with difficult cancer cases or frightened patients facing death, I read near-death experiences just as a reminder that the life we have on earth isn't the only life we'll get. It becomes clear to me that those who the NDErs meet on the other side seem interested in teaching us about love.

What is also striking about these accounts is that these lessons of love are not ones that come easily. They often force these heavenly explorers to understand love and other ideas that are not commonly encountered in our earthly lives. Near-death experiences reveal an idealized love that, they say, should be a goal even in this most imperfect world. NDErs often describe their frustration in their attempts to put the love they encountered in their experiences into practice. Often, they keep trying, even over the course of many years.

THE MEANING AND PURPOSE OF LIFE

What NDErs learn from their encounters has much overlap with issues surrounding the "meaning of life." They often give answers to questions humanity has wrestled with for millennia: Where were we before our birth? Why are we here on our earth? Where do we go after we die? The most recent version of the NDERF survey explores these questions. It asks "During your experience, did you encounter any specific information/awareness regarding earthly life's meaning or purpose?" The question was deliberately worded to ask about information that the NDErs received specifically *during* their experience and not at other times during their lives.

The 420 NDErs responding to this question answered as follows:

Yes	153	(36.4 percent)
Uncertain	43	(10.2)
No	224	(53.3)

Narrative responses were allowed to this question, and NDErs shared what they learned during their NDE about life's meaning and purpose. As with prior research of this type discussed in this book, I looked for both consistency and inconsistency in what NDErs shared in response to this question. Once again I was impressed with the remarkable consistency of the NDErs' responses.

In the NDEs shared with NDERF over the years, there are hundreds of NDEs with information about life's meaning and purpose, and they are strikingly uniform in what they have to say about it. This leads me to believe that what NDErs learned at death's door is vitally important for all of humanity.

The information that NDErs received during their experiences about life's meaning and purpose was predominantly in the form of general concepts. This should not be surprising, as it is very uncommon for NDErs to receive highly specific information during their NDEs about what they should or should not do in their earthly lives. For example, NDErs almost never encounter specific direction about what their vocation should be, who they should marry, and so on.

One of the most consistent and important concepts that NDErs learn is that our earthly lives *really are* meaningful and important. This is exceptionally good news in a world where so many people are at the point of despair over the belief that their lives could not possibly be meaningful and significant. Here is what the NDErs have to say:

- Everything is just as it should be. Life's situations aren't important—but rather, how we approach whatever is put before us. It's all about learning.[1]

- I know we are each here intentionally. We each have a purpose. We are needed.[2]

- Love one another.[3]

- We need to love and accept ourselves and each other. The actions and choices we make can be from either love or fear—love is golden light, fear is darkness.[4]

- Life is for living, not to impress someone or gain something. It is its own purpose.[5]

It is not surprising that many NDErs become aware that God is an important part of our earthly life's meaning:

- Since my experience, I believe that we are all created by a God of love to live a life of experience and then return to Him.[6]

- We have God to thank for every moment we spend on earth and with His gifts: family, children, and the earth's resources that He provided for us. He gave us everything.[7]

When NDErs share their understandings about life's meaning and purpose, among the most common insights have to do with *love*, as we have seen. Given the enormous importance of love, it is not surprising that NDErs found that love seems to be a foundation of our earthly life's meaning.

Helen D. was nine years old when she drowned and had her NDE. She found herself in the presence of beings who seemed *"unfamiliar,"* yet she felt as if she *"knew them somehow."* Helen had lots of questions for these beings, as many NDErs do. She was fortunate enough to be in their presence long enough to receive some excellent answers:

> *I had many questions after my initial panic had subsided. I wanted to know how the world worked, how it was made, what our purpose was in life, why we are here, and how we came to be here. They tried to slow me down; they said they couldn't answer everything for me at this time. They said that explaining would be difficult and that the answers are beyond us. But they did say that our purpose on this earth is to love, and that love is the purpose on earth—but sometimes humans have a hard time understanding this.[8]*

Other NDErs seem to echo Helen when they answered this question on the questionnaire about what life's meaning and purpose are:

+ Life's meaning or purpose is love. Clear and simple, love.[9]

+ To learn and understand love.[10]

+ Life is an opportunity for us to express and experience love. Only love is real.[11]

+ Unconditional love, and our job is to help one another find joy.[12]

+ The only thing that mattered was love.[13]

+ We take that love with us to the other side. People who worry about a loved one dying alone have nothing to worry about. We do not die alone.[14]

+ To overcome our fears, we need to love and accept ourselves and each other. The actions and choices we make can either be from love or fear—love is golden light, fear is darkness.[15]

The message given to NDErs is that we are here for a purpose and that love is very important to the meaning and purpose of our earthly lives.

RELATIONSHIPS

Many NDErs find that *relationships* with their loved ones are an all-important part of life's meaning and purpose. This is especially true of our relationships with children. Here are examples of what NDErs had to say regarding relationships in response to the survey question that asked NDErs directly about what gives life meaning and purpose:

+ I had to return for my loved ones, because they would suffer greatly without me. I had valuable work to complete yet, and this work would help humanity.[16]

+ I had to raise my child, and I should make my existence count.[17]
+ I felt confirmation that life's real meaning is love— for family and each other.[18]

Sometimes society doesn't seem to appreciate the enormous effort it takes to be a parent or caregiver for a family member. But the majority of NDErs find that these relationships are a very important part of life's meaning and purpose. A consistent message in NDEs is the importance of love in all of our earthly relationships.

"I'm So, So Sorry!"

Carol I. nearly died of complications of aplastic anemia, a serious disease of the bone marrow. She learned a great deal about the meaningfulness of relationships during her life review:

> *You could call it a "life review," but it was more in-depth than that—it was multifaceted. I experienced incidents from my life from three facets—all simultaneously: (1) from my own point of view, (2) from the point of view of whoever was with me, and (3) from the point of view of a witness, or watcher.*
>
> *One occasion I relived affected me deeply. I was in the eighth grade, and me and my friends were verbally abusing another one of our friends. It was cruel behavior, and I was drenched in the cruelty.*

I experienced that secret little thrill you get when you are cleverly mean to someone. I experienced the admiration, tinged with fear, of the girls who were going along with me. And I experienced the humiliation and pain of the girl we were torment- ing. I didn't just see her; I got to be her as she hud- dled next to the lockers, crying alone. I was full of remorse—over what I had done and also over the fact that I was dead and couldn't make up for it. My mind and my heart were crying out, "I'm sorry! I'm so, so sorry!"

This is a moving example of how unloving interactions hurt others. I can think of no better way to understand this than to experience the hurt from the other person's awareness.

Carol's NDE had a happy conclusion following her life review:

I heard a chuckle and felt a presence with me in the blackness. The presence expressed amusement over my despair and said, with heart and mind, something to the effect of: "You were just a kid. How bad could you have been?" Then I was embraced by love with layer upon layer of compassion. It felt like home! Like coming inside from the snow to a warm fire, the smell of good cooking, and the laughter of family. I was euphoric beyond anything I'd felt before or anything I've felt since.[19]

"The Earth Is Like a Big School"

A few NDEs are so remarkable that they are placed in a special section of the NDERF website called NDERF's Exceptional NDE Accounts.[20] Jean R.'s was one of these exceptional NDEs. Part of what made her NDE so special were the insights that she learned during her experience about relationships and other aspects of life's meaning and purpose:

> *My life review was all about my relationships with others. I felt what they felt in my relationship with them. I felt their love, and also their pain and hurt from things I had done or said to them. Their hurt made me cringe, and I thought, "Oh, I could have done better there." But mostly I felt love. No one was judging me; I felt no disapproval—only my own reactions to it all. The feeling of unconditional love saturating me continued; I was judging myself—no one else was judging me.*
>
> *I was told that the earth is like a big school, a place where you can apply spiritual lessons you have learned and test yourself to see whether you can "live" what you already know you should do. Basically, the earth is a place to walk the walk and live the way it should be done. It was made clear to me that some people come to the earth to work on one or more aspects of themselves, while others come to also help the world as a whole.*
>
> *The other side doesn't have the kind of pressures*

that the body imposes. Here on earth, we have to feed and clothe our bodies and provide shelter from the elements. We're under continual pressure to make decisions that have a spiritual base. We may be taught on the "other side" what we are "supposed to do," but can we live it under these pressures on earth?

From what I saw and heard on the other side, everything is about relationships and taking care of each other. We aren't expected to be perfect, but we are expected to learn. All of our experiences in a lifetime follow some sort of pattern, and we often learn the same lessons, but in a different way and under various circumstances. This is how we know what we are here to learn and test.[21]

CHAPTER 6

Judgment

Many NDErs receive some decision or what some might call a judgment from God or a heavenly being during their NDE. This can come in the form of being given a choice of whether to return to their earthly life or stay in heaven, or it may impart information about their lives or futures.

A CHOICE OR MANDATE

Of course, when many of us hear the word *judgment*, we may think of stories and medieval paintings in which God is either casting souls into hell or saving them for heaven. But this is rarely the context for the "judgments" people hear from God during their NDE. Judgments can be considered as things God has power over or as instances where individuals make conscious choices about their lives. Many people go through an exchange with God or a deceased loved one in which they make a choice to either live or die, are mandated to live, or are told to return to the land of the living.

"You Have a Decision to Make"

Lauren was riding a snow saucer that was being towed by a car. She struck a parked car while moving about 30 miles per hour. Her extensive injuries included five skull fractures, two broken eye orbits, a destroyed left cheekbone, and a jaw broken in three places.

> *I left my body and went into an aura of all white light. It was warm and peaceful, with pure Love emanating through and around me. My grandfather, who had passed away early that year, appeared to me and embraced me, saying, "My darling, you have a decision to make."*
>
> *I knew the decision was whether to stay or to go back.*
>
> *Then I had an opportunity to view my life. Everything seemed whole and complete. I knew my dog and cat would be taken care of, and I was pretty much willing to go, but I had some questions I wanted answered. I asked whether there would be anything wrong with me if I chose to go back.*
>
> *A voice answered, "No. The only thing that will show is the scar of the tracheotomy."*
>
> *"Will I remember this dream?"*
>
> *The voice said, "Yes, and if anyone asks you about the scar, you can share your experience."*

"If I choose to stay, what will be the cause of my death?"

"It will show that your spinal cord was severed."

"If I stay, what will become of me?"

"You will become the Light."

I remembered being in the Light and acknowledged the space, saying, *"The gift I am being given is to stay, but I can't accept the gift right now because my mother will grieve so greatly."* I saw that if I died, every time she fell into depression, she would sink deeper because of my death. The voice came back and said, *"So shall it be, and what you shall receive is a blessing."* At that moment I knew I was going to survive the accident.[1]

GOD DOES NOT JUDGE

Unlike what many imagine when they think of God's judgment on us, one common refrain we read in many NDEs is the idea that in God or in heaven there is "no judgment at all."

"No Judgment at All"

Having one near-death experience is a momentous life event, but Sharon had three NDEs. In one of her experiences she had important insights about judgment:

I was wrapped in rays of the sun and felt safe, secure, and peaceful—like I've never felt before. There was

*a beautiful garden and gorgeous music. I felt rocked
and cared for like a baby.*

*God was with me, holding me in His arms. I felt
this very clearly, and His love was within every fiber
of my being and every cell of my body. He was all
around me. I felt His total acceptance of me, with no
judgment at all. He is all love, completely love, and
He showered that love on me and through me.*

*I felt complete and whole for the first time ever.
I experienced a life review, which lasted only a blink
of an eye, and its lesson was that we judge ourselves;
God does not judge us. Then I experienced His voice,
which seemed to be infused into me, but I also heard
it. The messages were very clear: What you put into
the universe, you get back. Be very careful about the
words, thoughts, and actions that you put out into the
universe, because they will come back to you at some
point in your life. He told me to take these messages
back and share them with others.*[2]

Although Sharon experienced God as not judging
at all, she also learned that we judge ourselves and that
what we put out to the universe returns to us in some
way. This gives rise to the intriguing idea that, although
God might not serve as our judge, nonetheless there
might be a mechanism whereby judgment is built into
the universe's fabric. Could goodness and morality be
more like scientific laws than we suspected? It is a fascinating idea.

"Seeing Another Person's Heart"

Casper had an allergic reaction to medication and said, "*I could see my body lying on a stretcher as the ambulance attendants worked feverishly to save my life.*" Brooke shared this in her near-death experience:

> *In heaven, we have the privilege of seeing another person's heart as God sees it, so we can understand how someone might react differently to a situation than we would. In one scene, I saw someone who was very standoffish. After looking into their heart, I saw how they had been injured spiritually and acted harshly toward others out of fear. This made it easier for me to understand that not every action from another person is about me. Sometimes it's just about them.*[3]

"There Is No Condemnation"

Jill had a seizure during delivery. During her near-death experience she received messages that included awareness that there is no condemnation:

> *Every cell of my being was at peace, and I had the joy of loving myself and being loved the way I always wanted to be. One of my first revelations was that I was still me. It's hard to explain what a surprise and deep joy this was to me. I wasn't a mistake, and I was who I was always meant to be.*
>
> *Although I was still me, I could move through*

barriers without restriction. I saw and heard things that I can't remember, but I do recall the message, "There is no condemnation." God loves us, and we are all loved. And I remember the message that God is always taking care of me, so there is no reason to worry. The space between heaven and earth is only in our minds. We are able to join God and His life here on earth; we are one.[4]

Unconditional Love

In reviewing the God Study near-death experiences, I found that NDErs typically did not feel judged by God. Some examples of this are:

+ When I was enveloped in this clear white light, the love and acceptance of me was way beyond any love I have felt on earth. There was no judgment of me; there was only acceptance of me as a unique self.[5]

+ God does not judge anyone. He loves unconditionally.[6]

+ Powerful, unconditional love—the feeling of just knowing what it is. I felt like I was a sinner, and I was amazed that God would show me such love despite my mistakes in life that may have hurt others or myself.[7]

A lack of judgment is also typically seen in near-death experiences during the life review. It is very un-common that NDErs feel judged by another being even as they review their every action throughout their life.

It is occasionally reported that God expresses displeasure at the life of the near-death experiencer. For example, as we heard earlier from Bruce: "*God was not pleased by my life of alcohol and drugs. Several times I had almost died because of prescription drugs.*"[8]

God seems to know us more than we know ourselves. God knows our successes, failures, strengths, and shortcomings. As was discussed earlier, God seems to know *everything*. NDEs carry the message that God knows full well who we are, what we are, and still *loves us totally and unconditionally*. That is a message I find profoundly reassuring.

THE RETURN

Some of the most common exchanges that occur when NDErs meet God result in the person's being sent back to earthly life. They most commonly share that God told them to "go back" or "return" without much dialogue. NDErs understand that "going back" means returning to their earthly lives. They are often resistant to going back, but some embrace returning.

"I Was Not Going Back!"

Florene was about eight months pregnant, suffering from a complication, and rapidly losing blood when she had her NDE:

All of a sudden I was in the most beautiful place I have ever seen, looking into a beautiful "stream" of flowing blue water. The water was coming down off of a small cliff, and when it hit the ground, it sounded like the "ping" of fine crystal when you hit it with your fingernail. The colors were breathtaking—no artist could mix such colors. The stream was so deep it had no bottom, and even though I'm afraid of water, I knew I would be safe if I crossed the stream. There wasn't any sound except for birds and the sound of the water.

I was about to cross the stream when I was engulfed by a warm and bright light that felt like arms around me. The Light told me that I couldn't stay—I had much work left to do and I had to go back. I'm a stubborn person, so I argued with the Light, telling it that I was not going back!

I even stomped my foot—although I don't think I had a foot because it was like I was floating. After this experience I know that God has a beautiful sense to humor, because when I stomped my foot and said I didn't want to go back and that I was not going back, the Light smiled at me and chuckled and said, "Oh, yes you will." And of course I went back.[9]

"You Must Go"

Kim was in nursing school when she was riding an off-road motorcycle that crashed into a concrete flood-control channel:

I was inside a black void, with a sense of floating and complete silence and stillness. I felt panicked and afraid and knew that I was dead. I thought of all the things I wouldn't be able to attain—graduation, career, marriage, children—and felt surprised that I had died so young.

But once I noticed the stillness and peace, I became happy and intrigued. I thought that Jesus would come and take me. Then an unearthly white light appeared, and I "heard" a voice in my head. I knew this presence was "God," and I felt such peace and love. Then the voice told me that my time on earth wasn't done yet and I needed to go back. I pleaded to stay; I said I was fine with being dead and that I didn't want to go back. But the voice, "No, you must go."[10]

Reasons for Return

God also often communicates to near-death experiencers that "it is not their time." Again, NDErs typically understand that this means returning to their earthly lives. It is interesting that the afterlife is typically described as a realm where time does not exist, yet paradoxically it is still "not their time," and they must return to a realm where time does exist.

Occasionally there is dialogue about the return. Some NDErs hear from God that they "have a mission" or that they need to "do important work." Most of the time NDErs are returned to their earthly lives without being given a specific reason. Nor are they told specifically what to do when they return to their earthly lives. Occasionally the NDEr's dialogue with God includes awareness that return to earthly life is important for their family. Still others are offered a choice of whether or not to return.

Several near-death experiencers being sent back by God report hearing, *"I have given you a task that you have not finished,"* or having a sense that they had not yet fulfilled their purpose. These sorts of communications suggest a plan for our earthly lives with specific goals and purpose. It is notable that there are generally no details given regarding what these earthly objectives are. NDErs both in and outside of the God Study often become aware during their experiences that our earthly lives really are meaningful and filled with purpose.

When near-death experiencers are in the presence of God and there is a decision about their return to earthly life, they are usually sent back regardless of their desire to return. However, as we have seen, some NDErs are given a choice about returning to earthly life. It is unknown why some NDErs have such a choice and others do not.

"My Tasks Would Be Incomplete"

Elisa encountered God in her NDE and was given a choice to stay in the light or return. She was involved in a serious car crash and shared this:

I have never had such a spiritual and meaningful experience in all of my life. It was traumatizing and mind-boggling, but I carried God with me the whole time. I realized my purpose in life that day: to live every day like it is my last and always to let the love in my heart and soul flow freely. I realized that my life could be snatched away at any moment. I am much more fragile than I thought.

When I drifted in the light with God, at one point I begged him to take me with him. I told him that I didn't want to go back because it was safe with him. He asked me, "Are you finished?" Then I realized that I was not finished, and if I went home with the Lord, my tasks would be incomplete. He gave me a choice to stay or go, and I chose to go back and complete my unfinished business. He reminded me of my home and the indescribable and amazing beauty behind our reality. Now, pretty much every day, I crave my true home—because Heaven truly is my home. This earth is temporary, and time is an illusion that helps us understand being human.[11]

"If You Go In, You Cannot Come Out"

Viva also was given a choice. She had a complication during surgery. Viva was above her body on the operating table. The surgical team thought she was dead. As Viva shared, *"I became aware that I had a sheet over my whole body and head, that I was no longer in the surgical suite, and knew that they thought I was dead."* Here is her near-death experience:

> *I was standing in front of the most exquisite and beautiful English cottage—the perfect home. Golden light was streaming from the windows in the late dusk. I knew God was in the house, and I wanted to go inside to be with Him. As I put my hand on the door handle, I was told: "If you go in, you cannot come out. You have a four-year-old son who needs you. The people on earth need to know everything that you have witnessed—they need to know that their experience is not the totality of existence, but only a part of the overall plan." I understood that my fear was an obstacle to coming to know God and His presence, not only for me, but for everyone.*[12]

"Are You Finished?"

Near-death experiencers who choose between staying with God or returning to their earthly life are making a life-and-death decision that would be unimaginable to most of us. Stacy faced such a decision in his near-death experience. He became dehydrated and had a grand mal seizure:

> *A voice that came from everywhere—inside me, around me, back in time, forward in time—asked me: "Are you finished?" I instantly comprehended what it was asking: "Are you finished living in your body, on*

this material plane with the depressive self-disregard and emotional disdain for yourself and others that is interwoven throughout your being?" I knew that I couldn't stay in my body on this plane of existence and keep living this way. It was not the way of things, God's things, God's universe. The question was matter-of-fact: unemotional and nonjudgmental, loving and accepting. No blame, no shame, no guilt, no criticism, no anger—just a question. Are you finished?

I felt I had all the time there ever was to answer. My perception of time was an illusion of our material and bodily senses. I was totally relaxed, calm, and peaceful, and I knew I could comprehend and reach everything about my life. I was home in God's arms, and I was being given a peek at Universal Knowledge through the eyes of God. But then I remembered my wife; we weren't finished with our time together. She was waiting for me. I turned my head away from the tunnel, the light, and my grandparents and woke up in the hospital.[13]

Why Leave the Afterlife?

I reviewed eleven near-death experiences in which the NDErs were in the presence of God and were given a choice to stay in the afterlife or return to their earthly lives. I asked, "Why would anyone choose to leave a blissful afterlife?" The NDErs gave some interesting answers.

Five of the NDErs described choosing to return for the sake of their young children. One returned to be with his wife. A sixteen-year-old-girl said, "*God wanted me to go back and told me my purpose was not finished on this earth. I would have children. I wanted to do God's will. I told God I wanted to stay, but in my heart [my desire] to do his will was stronger.*"[14]

Another NDEr returned to her earthly body because she would have "*unfinished business and [her] tasks would be incomplete.*"[15] Yet another NDEr stated she was "*really worried about being out of [her] body and wanted to go back.*"[16]

God seemed to be encouraging several near-death experiencers to return to their earthly lives when given a choice. One NDEr shared, "*He reminded me of my home and the reality that really exists, and the beauty behind all of it is so indescribable and amazing.*"[17]

CHAPTER 7

Insight and Revelation

One of the more common things shared by near-death experiencers who encounter God is receiving some insight, special knowledge (or even all knowledge), or revelation. Sometimes NDErs simply "feel" or intuit this imparting of knowledge from God. Sometimes they encounter new vistas of knowledge that are impossible to fully recall when they return. But these "revelations," even when partial, may be transforming to those receiving them.

Take Loni, for example. She shared, "*I had undiagnosed Lyme disease for over a year. What most people don't know is that Lyme can attack your heart and simply stop it. I found this out the hard way while on a trip.*" Here is what happened during an NDE when she encountered God:

I asked Him, "What are we? How are we judged?"
And He showed me interwoven golden threads that

made me "me." But I didn't exist alone. My golden energy threads extended throughout the universe, and all humanity is woven together. We are all part of God's tapestry. (There really aren't any words to adequately describe this.)

But in between the golden threads He leaves empty spaces. He showed me that we can fill up these empty spaces with light or darkness during our lives. We are made of God, but we are given free will. And He knows how we spend that free will; there is no way to hide any of it.[1]

THE IMPORTANCE OF LEARNING

NDErs not only often receive knowledge; they may hear discussions on the importance of *acquiring* knowledge as a part of our earthly meaning and purpose. It seems important to value learning in our earthly lives. Here is what one NDEr had to say about this:

I was told that I was here to learn how to love and to gain knowledge. This wasn't said with words, but by thoughts, with all connotations of the words "love" and "knowledge" shown to me. I knew this wasn't just about book knowledge or physical love. It was about learning how to accept every race and have no prejudice; I was to keep expanding and learning about the earth, nature, animals, and people. And this was the mission of all humankind, not just me.[2]

Here are some of those simple gifts of the NDE as
told by those who have experienced them:

+ I was told why we are here and why we suffer. I was
  told we all have to live out lessons on earth for our
  souls to grow—like children learning new things.
  We suffer in order to learn how to cope with things
  and to develop our souls.[3]

+ Afterwards I thought that most things we worry
  about in life are pretty petty and unimportant.[4]

+ During the life review, I learned that selfishness
  needs to be eliminated from our earthly life.[5]

+ Life is for living, not for impressing someone or
  gaining something.[6]

+ I was very judgmental before my experience, which
  taught me that I have to let go of judgment and
  try to embrace each human being as the unique
  individual he or she is.[7]

+ The many things that we stress out about on earth
  don't matter; they are insignificant in light of the
  reality of space and out-of-body life.[8]

+ I learned that I hate most in others those qualities
  that I have in myself but can't see. I fit very neatly
  into all the areas I profess to hate in others. Love
  was the key to everything—acceptance and love.[9]

+ It seemed impossible to venture beyond a certain
  point while holding or harboring any negative,
  unloving feeling.[10]

Underlying many of these reports is the assumption that everything in life is meaningful, that we are to learn from our successes and learn from our failures. Even in the difficult times life seems to be meaningful.

What is meaningful to us is a foundation of who we are. It reflects our values and directs our life efforts. NDEs suggest that it is ultimately our decision to decide what is meaningful to us in our lives and how we live our lives in response to these values. Taking these reports from heaven seriously would suggest that it would be reasonable to consider what NDErs teach us about love for our journey to grow spiritually and draw closer to God.

"A Connection and Harmony with Existence"

Jeremiah experienced his special connection with God during a near-death experience. Jeremiah was having surgery to repair a hernia when complications of the surgery caused his heart to stop. Here are Jeremiah's comments about his NDE:

> Until this experience, I didn't have a clue what happens when we die. It was an open question for me. I believed in God, but I didn't think anyone or any religion had a clue. Now I'm forever changed. I now understand that the universe in its entirety is God and all connected. There is a connection and harmony with existence, but there is no absolute knowledge. But God does exist. I was personally in his/its presence and fully conscious. God Is. It doesn't matter

if one believes or not. God simply Is. The oneness is God; it is all one in the same. God is all around us and in us on this earthly plane as well.[11]

"I Am Your Sister"

Sandy was five years old when she developed an inflammation of the brain called encephalitis from a mosquito bite and nearly died. In her NDE, she not only learned about a sister she never knew she had, but she also received information from her sibling's angel about the future:

> *"I died" and drifted into a safe, black void of comfort and ease, where I felt right at home. I felt no pain and wasn't afraid. In the distance I saw a small light that was drawing me toward it. I felt myself rushing to this light. When I got to the light, I knew it represented peace and joy, but most of all a deep unconditional love.*
>
> *The light was a sparkling, glowing cloud. I heard a voice in my head and knew it was God. We never talked about God at my house, and I never went to church, but I knew it was God. And I knew that this place, with this beautiful light that was God was my real home. I was surrounded by the light and one with it. It was like being scooped up and held safe by my daddy when a dog was barking at me, only more so.*
>
> *Then we were joined by another, smaller light.*

It was a girl who was about ten years old, and she looked a little like me. She recognized me, and we hugged. "I am your sister," she said. "I was named after our grandmother Willamette; our parents called me Willie. They were waiting to tell you about me later when you were ready."

We talked together without using any words. She kissed me on the head, and I felt her warmth and her love. Then she told me that I had to go back to save mother from a fire. "You need to go back now, Sandy; this is very important."

"No, I don't want to," I said, "let me stay here with you."

But she repeated gently, "Mother needs you to save her from the fire."

I cried and threw a temper tantrum like a little brat. I fell on the ground and sobbed and thrashed around.

I could see my parents, kind of like a movie, sitting beside my hospital bed, begging me not to die. I was very sad for them, but I still wasn't ready to give up the beauty and awesome feelings of all that was good about this place, this heaven. God chuckled at my childish antics and looked at me with great compassion.

He then pointed a finger at another light that was forming in the distance. That light became our next-door neighbor Glen. Glen was a kindly old man who loved kids and invited us over to play with his dogs and give us treats. His wife, Rose, eventually would tell us all to go home, but Glen would scold her and say, "Rose, never tell Sandy she has to go. She can stay as long as she wants." But here, the light that was Glen shouted at me, "Sandy, go home! Go home now!" It was such a shock when he yelled at me that I stopped fighting and felt a little embarrassed about my behavior. I quit crying and was back in my body in an instant.

It turns out that the day after I went into the hospital, Glen died suddenly of a heart attack. I learned of his death only after I told my story to my parents.

When I told them the story, they at first called it a dream. But then I drew a picture of my "angel sister." My parents were shocked and confirmed that their daughter Willie had died of accidental poisoning about one year before I was born. They had decided not to tell my brother or me about her until we were able to understand what life and death were about.

As far as the need to rescue my mom from a fire, none of us has a clue about that. But when my mom was helping me write this, I asked her what her life would have been like if I had died. She replied, "I cried for months after Willie left us. If we had lost you too, it would have been like a living hell, fire and all."[12]

UNIVERSAL KNOWLEDGE

During their experiences, NDErs frequently become aware of enormous and all-encompassing knowledge that has been referred to as *universal knowledge*. They are generally unable to remember all of the knowledge that they encountered. Here's what NDErs have to say about this:

+ I was suddenly amazed that I knew everything there was to know, even reflecting to myself, "So *that's* how it works."[13]

+ In that state of total recall, I became one with all life, part of a collective consciousness, and I knew everything. It was not an intellectual knowledge, like knowledge you acquire from studying facts. I knew because I had experienced being everything.[14]

+ I felt like I could understand everything if I chose to. It was like everything was right there. I was like an enormous buffet that had every kind of fruit, vegetable, cheese, bread, and all I had to do was reach for whatever I wanted.[15]

+ I felt I was given all the answers; only when I popped back into my body, I lost most of it.[16]

+ It was like I was a computer and receiving an endless download of knowledge. I asked questions and received answers immediately. Anytime I posed a question, the answer was presented.[17]

Sometimes NDErs bring back fragments of knowledge that they recall later in life. I have to smile when I read accounts like this:

Sometimes the universal knowledge I gained during my NDE pops into my head as things occur in the world. For instance, when the story about a black hole in our galaxy hit the papers last week, I blurted out spontaneously, "It's about time they figured that one out!" Of course everyone looked at me like I was nuts, but I just shrugged my shoulders and said "old news."[18]

NDErs have described learning about science, mathematics, physics, and far more. In my early years of NDE research I eagerly read each NDE that told of encountering specialized knowledge, hoping there would be some nugget of unearthly understanding to share with the world. It never happened. NDErs generally cannot retain the universal knowledge they were given when they return to their earthly life. It seems to be like trying to put an ocean of knowledge in the teacup of our brain—as if the knowledge "overflows" and cannot be retained.

The most recent version of the NDERF survey asked, "Did you have a sense of knowing special knowledge or purpose?" Reponses from 420 near-death experiencers were as follows:

Yes	195	(46.4 percent)
Uncertain	50	(11.9)
No	175	(41.7)

Review of the narrative responses to this question suggests that there is vast knowledge waiting for us in the afterlife.

"I Knew All Things"

Jennifer delivered her baby, then began bleeding heavily. She coded twice and was pronounced dead. But Jennifer recovered from her harrowing close brush with death and shared a remarkable NDE with insights about knowledge and the afterlife:

Suddenly I was aware of having infinite knowledge—I knew everything, all languages, all religious thought—all at once. I was one with the Creator and with Creation itself. I was the Creator. We all were; those who haven't come back still are. It's impossible to describe.

My earthly body, the container or vessel of my soul, had been shed. I was God along with everyone else, and yet God was still a universal power that was gentle and kind, humble and pure. God lives in me; the soul of God was breathed into my dead body when I chose to live. We were in and through and with each other. It was humbling, beautiful beyond beauty, and powerful in the most gentle and kind way.

Everything seemed to be clear—languages, death and life, God, Creation, love, peace, joy, sorrow. I knew the infinity, oneness, flexibility, and omniscience of all beings; I knew that our physical bodies separate us from the One that we are. We are like water poured from a pitcher into individual glasses, where we stay until we die and return to the whole. The purpose I received was to circulate this knowledge—the knowledge that love is the purpose, or that the purpose of love is life.[19]

"Everything I Have Ever Needed"

Romy was a Buddhist living in Israel. Her family was driving in India when their car went off the road and tumbled down a mountain. She had a detailed near-death experience that included the following:

The light that I encountered felt supreme—unending, unconditional, immense love, a force that feels eternal, powerful, and creative at the same time. This satisfies my definition of "God."

I was sitting near the source of the light and felt it strongly. It was everything. Everything I have ever needed, everything I need or everything I might ever need in the future. Everything was in this warm, immensely healing and nourishing light. It was pure, immense, powerful unconditional Love. I knew I could trust this light.[20]

"I Would . . . Know Everything"

Demi, whom we met earlier, was fourteen years old when she was caught in an undertow while swimming in the ocean. She shared this from her near-death experience:

I didn't see a Godlike being, but there was a power there that has been described as God. This energy communicated with me and gave me very specific messages.

I felt totally at one with this energy. I felt like I was the energy source and was communicating with myself, but I knew it was a much higher power that I was a part of. I knew that all knowledge was in the light and that, once there, I would be and know everything. Entering it would be like going home, only magnified a billion times. I was comforted, accepted, loved, and totally connected with the supreme energy force.[21]

"No Limits on the Power of God"

James was a physician who was legally blind. A cardiac catheterization error led to a heart attack, congestive heart failure, and the loss of his heartbeat and blood pressure for about four minutes. Although blind, he declared, "I could see clearly without glasses. I could see distant and near without restrictions. In this world I am legally blind even with glasses." James encountered God in his NDE:

Eventually, I reached an area of darkness with a faint light in the distance. I felt a strong compulsion to travel to the light. As I neared it, I became aware of other spirits or souls around me. I couldn't see them, but I sensed them. A mixture of clouds, fog, smoke, and mist was connected with the spirits and the light. I saw the hazy outlines of indistinct figures and knew them. I was communicating with them, but not with words. We just did it—instantaneous thought transmitted with them.

I met my sister and my mother, who had both died years ago. I was happy to be with them, but I kept being drawn to the light—the most brilliant and bright golden white light that permeated everything.

As I got closer to it, I felt an overwhelming power and presence that I recognized as God. I asked questions and got the answers immediately. I was filled with love, joy, and happiness and was surrounded by unconditional love, forgiveness, and acceptance. I wanted to keep going through the light but received a message that clearly said, "No, go back. It isn't your time." The message was accompanied by visions of my wife and children. I didn't want to go back, but I didn't get a choice and awoke with a doctor shaking me.

The light and the presence of the entity were clearly God. It was present everywhere and a part of everything. There were no limits to the power of God.[22]

"God Sent Me Back *Well*!"

As a physician, I am interested in near-death experiences in which encounters with God are associated with a healing that is beyond any medical explanation. Many say that God is the greatest physician, and I reflected on this when reading Nancy's NDE. She had a case of lupus that was so severe she bled into her lungs. Nancy had oxygen deprivation so damaging that she developed brain injury. A scan showed she had no brain function. She was disconnected from the ventilator she was on and should have died. When Nancy recovered, she shared her remarkable NDE:

> When I was disconnected from the respirator, I was suddenly in a dimly lit room by myself. The room had a door that I knew was special. Then I became aware that I was no longer alone. God was there too!—an all-encompassing presence—complete, total, and unconditional love in its highest form! I didn't see any figure, but I had no doubt that this was God. Then He spoke to me, with such compassion, and said "Are you too tired?"
>
> I knew that He was asking me whether I was too tired to go through that door—which would be my death. I don't remember my answer, but I do know I was given a choice whether or not to go back. So it must have been my choice to come back, and miraculously, God sent me back well! After so many years of suffering with the pain of lupus, when I came back, my lupus was completely gone! Since my NDE, all tests for lupus have been negative.

Although physicians are reluctant to use the term

miracle, I am unable to call what happened to Nancy anything other than a miracle. As Nancy went on to say:

> I was surrounded by the unconditional love of God, and it was so much greater than human love. The most meaningful part of the experience was receiving the sure knowledge that God is real and loves me unconditionally—that He is love.[23]

REVELATIONS ABOUT THE FUTURE

Several NDErs received information about their future during their NDE. Although this sounds sensational, in many cases the information serves as comfort and encouragement for their return to earthly life. It is uncommon for people to receive detailed information about the future, though a few encountered this in their NDE.

"He's Not the One"

In this NDE, a woman named Priscilla goes into anaphylactic shock and becomes *"just a soul, not a body"* and briefly encounters God, who gives her a hint of her future, but only a hint:

> I died and flew out through my body, down through the ER bed, and up into a corner of the room. It was pitch black, like a total void, and I felt wonderful, with no pain. I felt light, like I had no body. I knew that God or some higher power was there and that

He had the key to my going back to earth. I didn't talk to God, and He didn't talk to me—it was all emotions.

I demanded that I return because my four children needed me. I also insisted that I had to help my mother, who was eighty and had already lost one child. Then God laughed, not at me, but because I was so angry with Him. He "told" me that I could go back because my requests were all for others.

Then I saw my boyfriend outside the building—he had broken up with me the day before. "Someone" told me: "Don't be upset. He's not the one." Then I was back in my body.[24]

"I Had a Long Time to Go"

Christopher was nearly crushed to death and suffocated at age eight when his brothers "dogpiled" on him. After leaving his body and seeing the dog pile from above, Christopher described going to a heavenly realm and meeting with an angel who told him it was not time for him to die. Here is his description of the event:

I was at the bottom of the dog pile, and my lungs were hurting and my breath was getting short. I closed my eyes and prayed I would get through it. Then suddenly, I could breathe again. I opened my eyes and saw the dog pile from above, with my body twitching underneath it. I looked around and found myself eye to eye with the gutters of the roof of the house. I was surprised—and kind of excited—that I was that high up. I looked down and saw that the boys had gotten off of me and were looking concerned. Then I felt a tug at my back and was in a dark tunnel with a clear bright light at the end of it.

I was fascinated at first, but then I started worrying that I wouldn't be able to leave. I called out to anyone, and the light at the end of the tunnel became blinding. I closed my eyes and covered my face with my arms.

A guy's voice asked me whether I was okay, and I lowered my arms and looked up. I was in the middle of a meadow, with rolling hills and beautiful flowers all around. I could see cottages in the distance. I heard beautiful music in the background. The air emanated love and warmth—a love that goes deep into the soul and can withstand anything.

The guy called me by name, and I turned around. There was a young man with longish blond hair and blue eyes, dressed in the whitest clothing I've ever seen. He towered over me, and looking down on me with love and concern, he said that I wasn't supposed to be here. I asked him why, and he said I had a long time to go before I could enter heaven and stay. I wondered to myself how long, and he answered me as if he had heard what I was thinking: "You are supposed to be eighty-three years old before you get here."[25]

CHAPTER 8

Heaven

Many near-death experiencers describe visits to a heavenly realm. We have already seen many examples of this throughout this book. In addition, most NDErs who report an encounter with God describe that it occurred in a realm that could reasonably be called *heavenly*. Many people find these powerful descriptions of heaven the strongest messages of hope in near-death studies, especially for those who are ill or filled with anxiety. But our focus here is not pastoral; it is to survey what we can learn about this realm from these reports.

Encounters with God almost always take place in a heavenly realm that may consist of a variety of common earthly elements, including mountains, valleys, forests, streams, lakes, rivers, and dwellings. Often they are described as having a decidedly unearthly appearance (often due to color or brightness or scale). There can also be vast cities that may be beautiful beyond anything on earth.

Typically this place is associated with feelings of peace, love, and connection in the environment. Beautiful or "indescribable" music is reported. Sometimes spiritual beings or angels are present. The importance of learning or gaining knowledge is also often in evidence, and there are frequent reports of seeing or experiencing institutions of learning (sometimes called "temples of knowledge"). People also often describe receiving knowledge directly in the form of telepathic exchange from Light Beings.

+ I saw beautiful gardens and places to rest.[1]

+ I had a complete sense of awe and beauty stamped upon my mind.[2]

+ I was not on earth. I saw only the clouds and the light.[3]

+ I entered a room that was so beautiful and bright that I was blinded with colors.[4]

+ The field of grass was absolutely beautiful! Turquoise is my favorite color now.[5]

+ The place where I was, it was like no place on earth, with beautiful and new, and full of happiness.[6]

+ It was a paradise, a beautiful forest.[7]

The NDERF case studies contain hundreds of descriptions of this mystical place called heaven. Notice I did not say "mythical." To call it mythical would imply that it's not real or is a made-up place, which would be disrespectful to those who have given the accounts we have been studying. To the probable millions of people around the world who experienced it during their near-death experiences, heaven is a very real place, an authentic destination. Since so many people have described it with consistency, regardless of their religion, we need to study their accounts carefully.

When I hear these consistent descriptions of heaven presented by those who, before their experience, identified with various religions, I am reminded of the Greek philosopher Epictetus's maxim: "All religions must be tolerated . . . for every man must get to heaven in his own way."

The heavenly realm is often a space where NDErs encounter God. Again, as we have seen repeatedly already, this heavenly realm is usually linked with encountering or feeling an unearthly love and overwhelming joy:

+ I have never felt loved by someone on this earth the way I felt loved by this being.[8]

+ I felt the most beautiful feeling of love and belonging.[9]

+ I felt someone was carrying me very lovingly—an unconditional love.[10]

+ The very air emanated love and warmth, a love that goes deep into the soul and can withstand anything.[11]

- ◆ I felt complete love, joy, and peace, like a warm blanket wrapped around me on a cold morning.[12]
- ◆ I felt a love I have never felt before.[13]

In my research, I found that NDErs generally experience the heavenly realm in three different ways, with some overlap: (1) as an overwhelmingly beautiful place; (2) as a boundary between life and death; or (3) as a meeting place with God, spirits, or deceased loved ones.

HEAVEN'S BEAUTY

NDErs who visit the heavenly realm frequently report the types of beauty one sees on earth. They tell of beautiful forests, streams, mountains, and deserts. But there are some stark differences between what we see on earth and what is reported in heaven. NDErs who have been there often talk about a landscape that seems to be lighted from within. They talk about a world full of "hypercolors," ones they have never seen or can't describe. As one NDEr wrote, *Everything was more bright and vivid. Down here it's like an old black-and-white TV. Up in Heaven it's hi-def, 3-D, big-screen TV.*[14] These kinds of visions may be called "vistas of heaven":

- ◆ Everything was sharper; colors were clearer and more vibrant. My field of view was completely open. All the colors were unearthly beautiful. I have hearing loss in my life; I did not have that in death, and I could hear much better than ever in my life. The sounds were beautiful and melodic. I was completely filled with emotions such as great joy; deep, deep love; comfort; gratitude; freedom; an *"everything* is as it should be" feeling. [15]

+ I was amazed at how much more real and vibrant the colors and light around me were. There was a strong feeling that *this* was real, and that my body was just a coat I had been wearing. It felt good to be out of it. I felt free from pain, confusion, and all the heaviness of the weight of life on my shoulders. My entire perspective on life was changing as fast as I could think. I basked in the wonder of it all. [16]

"A Crystal City"

The heavenly realm can be found in city form. NDErs may report going to a city of gleaming buildings and bright lights, a "crystal city," as many call it, which may be peopled with spiritual or angelic beings. Here is one such example.

Randall was six years old and playing in the back of a garage with a car that was running. His heart stopped from the carbon monoxide poisoning that occurred. Here is his near-death experience:

> I went quickly through a tunnel and was met by two shimmering beings who stayed with me the entire time. They took me to a crystal city where everything was vibrant and alive. They showed me different rooms in the crystal city.

One of the rooms was the room of knowledge. There, I knew all there is to know about everything. But the beings didn't let me keep all that knowledge. The next room was like a giant hall. I was told that all the great healers of the world were there, and I was among them. The next room was the shape of an octagon and had a well in the middle of the floor.

When I looked into the well, I saw what seemed to be moving and churning energy—like confetti that was all the colors of the rainbow. I put my hands into the well and felt the energy of it. It felt like static electricity and heightened all my senses. Then four tunnels suddenly appeared in front, behind, and to the sides of me; they had light at the ends of them. The two beings conveying to me that I had to go, but I could choose which path to take.[17]

"Up a Long Winding Staircase"

Another NDEr shared a similar experience of heaven as a city. Depressed and tired of the treatment and medication she had to endure to cope with the depression, this woman decided to commit suicide. She went to a mountain trail, and started consuming a "stockpile of pills" and vodka. She called her sister to tell her she was hiking with a friend and would see her possibly in the next several days. Eighteen hours later her sister found her in the deep woods. She awoke briefly in the hospital, where doctors and nurses were struggling to keep her alive. She left her body, and then ...

> *I was in a strange, unearthly city where three young women—all beautiful and glamorous, as I wanted to be—took me to a white building on the other side of the city. We went up a long winding staircase to a loft that was filled with light. A man came in and made various motions with his hand and spoke almost to himself—and I understood that he was transforming me into a physically beautiful woman.*
>
> *We left the building and went outside where the light was bright and clear and snow was all around—but it wasn't cold. Eventually, I decided I needed to go. I didn't know where I was supposed to go, but I had a strong feeling that I was late for something and I had to leave.*
>
> *The three women accompanied me to the edge of another city, which was very busy and had lots of tall buildings. Lots of people were there—traveling together in small groups and all looking happy. Then a young man caught my attention because he was sitting alone and looked very unhappy. Of all the people I could see, he was the only one who looked unhappy. I wanted to go talk to him, but the leader of the three young women told me I shouldn't disturb him. There was a specific reason I wasn't supposed to bother him, but I don't remember it anymore. Then I realized that he was my stepbrother who had committed suicide a few years before.*

> *The young women told me that they couldn't go with me in the direction I wanted to go—which was the opposite direction of all the people. I had to go alone. I felt compelled to go, although no one or no thing told me I should. I knew that it was my choice and nothing was influencing my choice. I didn't know where I was going, but if I would just go, I would get where I needed to be. So I left.*[18]

"A Magnificent City Sparkling in the Sun"

In this account the NDEr has to face the choice of going into a city of light and staying in heaven or returning to earth. As a teenager, Mike W. had an accident while riding down a hill on a push bike. He had an "enthusiasm for speed" at that point in his life and decided to go fast down a steep hill. He lost control of his bike at the bottom of the hill and landed on his head on a curb. A woman who witnessed the accident called 911 and could not find Mike's pulse. Mike tells the rest of the story:

> *I was standing in a place out of this world on the side of a gently sloping hill. The grass was flat on the hill as if it had been windswept for years. Was this heaven?*
>
> *I realized that I wasn't alone. Someone dressed in brilliant white stood beside me. The sky was dark behind me and to either side, but there was light in front of me—over the top of the hill—a brilliant white light like the sun rising in the morning that*

made me feel like I was glowing inside. The person beside me, perhaps an angel, took me by the hand, and we slowly walked up the hill together. The light shining beyond the top of the hill became brighter as we neared it.

The next moment I was watching various scenes of my past, present, and future life. My life was replayed before me like I was watching a three-dimensional movie. Each scene was exactly how it happened and was real. I had plenty of time to reflect on my life story right up to my present age of fifteen, yet it didn't seem to take any time at all. I felt very exposed watching all this, but the person next to me didn't judge me; I seemed to judge myself instead.

Then we reached the top of the hill and were poised on the edge of a chasm. Looking out over the edge I could see a magnificent city sparkling in the sun as though it was made of diamonds—like something from a fairy tale. The person in white asked me whether I wanted to enter heaven—the holy city. If I did, I could never return to the earth or my family. Or did I want to go back into my physical body on earth?

I would have loved to stay there in that wonderful place. I knew that I was made for this. But I could also see glimpses of my family crying and praying for me. My heart was divided. I wanted to enter heaven, but I also sensed that God had a plan for me, so maybe I should return to earth.[19]

INEFFABLE MUSIC

When NDErs encounter heavenly music, very few, if any, are able to recreate to their satisfaction the beautiful unearthly melodies they heard during their NDEs.

Yet despite its ineffable quality, this music may have a powerful effect on NDErs. In my experience I see it enticing NDErs to remember what was so good in their experience, and pushing them to recall the messages of their NDE and their visit to the heavenly realm.

"The Most Heavenly Music"

At the age of twelve, Erwin V. was in a near-fatal traffic accident that left him in a coma for nine days. After floating through a tunnel that left him feeling a deep calm, Erwin went on to hear an ineffable music. Here is how he described the experience:

> I heard the most heavenly music ever played. At first, I was afraid, but then I felt calm and happy, with no pain at all. Somehow I received the message that I had to return, since this life wasn't yet fulfilled. At that moment I floated back through the dark tunnel.
>
> I woke up in my body and cried out in pain. I was sorry I had returned because I longed for the calm feeling I had in the tunnel, and no pain.
>
> After nine days I woke up and saw my parents. My dad was so happy and said that I could have anything as a welcome-back gift. I asked him for a

guitar, because I wanted to produce that heavenly music. Later, I learned how to play the bass guitar and had my own band for ten years. That music I heard has always remained very important in my life.[20]

"The Halls of Music"

Edna's near-death experience took place a result of a complication of childbirth. She suffered a terrible pain in her chest, a sinking feeling, and unconsciousness. She had an out-of-body experience as part of her NDE that put her next to the ceiling and able to look down at her physical body and the medical staff who were attending to it. Then she says:

I went down a blue tube with a bright light at the bottom. When I exited the tube, I was surrounded by the most wonderful music—similar to pan pipes—that was everywhere. The feeling was so peaceful and there was no pain. I asked, "Where am I?" and was told, "The Halls of Music."

There were a lot of people, and they were all exuding so much love. The sky was a wonderful blue and the grass so green. I saw a bridge and wanted to cross it, but I couldn't—there was some kind of invisible barrier.

Someone I felt I knew appeared on the other side of the bridge, and he said, "It's not time yet. You still have work to do." I wanted so much to stay, but in no time I was back in my body.[21]

"Music I Had Never Heard the Likes Of"

Nan should have died from the overdose of medication that she took. Her consciousness traveled out the top of her head. Guided by two beings, she zoomed toward a pinpoint of light that became larger and larger:

> *As we got close to the light I saw tens of thousands of beings dressed in white gowns all facing the Light and singing music I had never heard the likes of before. They were in the service of The Light and apparently "singing" praises to The Light. The Light was filled with the most extraordinary, overwhelming, and indescribable feeling of love.*[22]

From the light came a male voice that ordered her to *"go back"* to her earthly existence, because she had a great deal to learn. With that, Adrian reluctantly felt herself returning to herself, as her consciousness returned to her body through her head.

The inability to recreate that heavenly sound may be a source of frustration for many who have exposure to what truly must be out-of-this-world music. Many of the NDERF case studies discuss the ineffable quality of the music NDErs hear during their visit to heaven. It is as though the music is too beautiful to forget, yet too perfect to recreate.

HEAVEN AS A BOUNDARY BETWEEN LIFE AND DEATH

NDErs may discover a location that serves as an in-between place, or boundary. Some may see something that seemingly serves as the entrance to heaven. Heaven may be presented as a place they will not yet enter before they return to the earthly realm. There may be a boundary in the form of a barrier that keeps them from doing that. It usually appears as a physical object—a bridge, perhaps, or a stream or a stand of trees—but it may also be an area with no physical markers. NDErs are often drawn to the barrier because it will take them farther toward the heavenly landscape. A being with them may make them aware that by crossing that barrier they will no longer be able to return to their earthly life.

Some NDErs are told not to cross the barrier by the being because they "have more to accomplish" or "are needed" back on earth. Other NDErs decide for themselves not to go past the barrier.

"The Gate Wouldn't Open"

For Kerry L., heaven was such a place. Depression caused her to take a handful of sleeping pills and leave a note saying she didn't want to live anymore. When her sister found Kerry nearly comatose, she called an ambulance. On the way to the hospital Kerry could hear someone saying that they "were losing her." Shortly thereafter, she slipped into darkness. Kerry tells her story:

Everything was so dark, and I was being whisked through a tunnel at great speed. Then there was the brightest, most blinding light I have ever seen, and I was floating above a field of flowers. I saw beautiful pearly gates and wanted to go through them so badly. But the gates wouldn't open; I could only look over them. Everything on the other side was more beautiful than anyone could imagine. The roads were emerald, and diamonds and gold were everywhere. Everything was breathtakingly shiny and sparkly.

I saw Our Heavenly Father. He looked ghostly, but had a bright whitish glow about him. I kept saying, "I need to get in there, I need to go to heaven. Let me in, let me in." And He replied: "You can't get in here. It's not your time to go."

Then he disappeared and everything went backward, back through the flowers, the bright light, the tunnel, and the darkness.

Kerry's NDE had a strong effect on her. She wrote that she sometimes has a *"sixth sense"* about future events, that *"things just pop into [her] head like something is going to happen, and it does."* Kerry wrote:

This NDE completely changed my life. I was no longer afraid to die, and I was more aware of a higher being. I knew that God had something more in store for my life. I just didn't know what at the time. Now

I have a daughter in college and a beautiful grand-daughter. And that in itself is a beautiful thing.[23]

HEAVEN AS A MEETING PLACE

Many NDErs who enter a heavenly space encounter loved ones who have passed away.

"Several of My Relatives Were There"

Margaret B. was at work when she had a brain seizure that led to a cardiac arrest. She found herself outside her body high in the corner of the room watching the paramedics perform CPR in an attempt to get her heart started. Then she wrote that she had a *"sensation sort of like falling backwards."* She then had an NDE that led to a choice to stay in heaven or cross a barrier and return to her earthly life. Here is her story:

> *Bright light was all around, and then I saw my grandmother. Suddenly we were at a meadow, and in the distance were trees and lots of people. Near to us was a large flat boulder, with a small creek running past it and beyond where we stood. Several of my relatives were there also, and we talked a lot about things in my life and the fact that somehow I wasn't doing something I needed to do.*
>
> *I had all this "happy peace" and wanted to stay there, but when I told them that, they said I needed to go back. I wasn't done. My grandfather told me quite gently*

that I had to cross the creek and finish my work. Everyone was so gentle, but also insistent that I cross back over the creek. Eventually, they won out. The next thing I remembered was being wheeled to the ambulance.[24]

"I Knew This Heavenly Personage Was Jesus"

Here is a story from an anonymous NDEr who met Jesus in a heavenly realm:

A bright mist permeated everything. The light was everywhere; it even passed through me! I looked at my hand and the light passed right through it! My hand was transparent, but that didn't surprise me.

I walked with a heavenly personage. His countenance shone with a brightness I can't describe. I knew this heavenly personage was Jesus.

We weren't walking in the physical sense; it was more like we were floating, with bare space between us and the ground. Everything was white and bright— the plants were so bright green and the water was sparkling clean. A bright glow surrounded everything.

I wanted to take a drink from the stream that was running through the garden we were walking through. When I tried to scoop up the water in my hands, it literally ran through my hands, and my hands weren't wet. Jesus stopped walking and looked at me while I was trying to drink this water. I could feel his eyes on me. And my thirst was gone, even though I wasn't able to drink the water.

When this heavenly being and I talked, we didn't do it with our mouths, but we were communicating. His countenance shone, and how he felt about me shone from Him. He exuded love and concern and caring for me. The feeling of peace was indescribable.

I was given the choice to either go back to earth and live more life or stay with Him in heaven. He knew that I didn't want life on earth if it meant being trapped in an unresponsive body unable to communicate. The look of love in His eyes filled my heart with joy.[25]

"All Have Their Seed from Heaven"

Another NDEr who experienced heaven as a meeting place is Diane C., whose experience in heaven began in 1958 when she thought her water broke during her fourth pregnancy, only to find that she was really hemorrhaging. She called her husband at work, who rushed home to find that she had bled through two mattresses and onto the floor. Her husband picked her up and loaded her into the car. By the time they arrived at the hospital, she stated that she had already died. Here in her own words is her amazing story in which she meets an angel and God. We pick up where Diane encounters heaven:

Words are inadequate to describe Heaven. But I knew I was home. I knew this was where I'd come from. I first came to a serene and beautiful country-

side filled with animals—they were so beautiful and contented, so full of love. The grass and trees and flowers were all so exquisite, and a vibration of love flowed back to me from them. The water was living and sparkled back to me with love. I heard music all around, fully more melodic and more beautiful than anyone could write on this earth, just suddenly playing and filling my soul with joy.

Everything was richer and more beautiful than anything we could ever create on earth. I realized that everything we create that is beautiful—all paintings, woven rugs, tapestries, carvings—all have their seed from Heaven. We saw all this before we came to earth, and we try to recapture some of Heaven while on earth. We deeply desire Heaven on earth. We miss it deep in our souls.

An angel took me to view the reflection of God's Light—not the full force of His Awesome Wonder. I was so filled with love and wanted to hug Him with joy. His voice came into my mind, and He commanded me to stretch out my hands and arms so that I could see I was made of solid light. And then He imparted the knowledge that we all are made of solid light, and we each have our own identity and purpose. Each of us was created before we entered earth, and each was male or female before that entry. He contains both sides, and this is the truth of it. For it is not the sexual side, but the strong and the gentle *of both sides of Him that determine who we will be—a balance of His being.*

I have a peace most people don't have about death because I know that is what Christ meant by the words, "Unless you are born again, you cannot enter into the Kingdom of Heaven." They have nothing to do with the meaning religion has given them; they are about something we all must do.

Our Father told me that I had to go back to earth and complete my test; there was much I still needed to do. He affirmed that He loved me and would be with me all my life.

On that sad day, Diane told the doctor what had happened during her cardiac arrest. Her doctor couldn't relate to her experience, but her priest could. Diane felt she now "had the keys to the Kingdom of Heaven." Diane has never forgotten the lessons she learned in heaven.

In her NDERF case study she wrote about what she learned:

It is about love. We must love ourselves, and in this way we love God. He is within each of us. We then can love others, even our enemies. We are here to love life, to live life, and to express back to our Creator our joy at having life here and seeing how beautiful our world is regardless of how we make it. We need love, and with it we receive faith, hope, and confidence to get through life.[26]

SHARED EXPERIENCES OF HEAVEN

Sometimes, encounters in heavenly realms are shared experiences in which NDErs meet other people having a near-death experience.

"My Grandmother Stayed"

In the Netherlands, Karen had two life-threatening events within a short time of each other. This is an exceptionally rare example of two shared NDEs occurring sixteen days apart. Karen's grandmother had a stroke and was unconscious during Karen's first NDE. During Karen's second NDE her grandmother died at the same time. It was clear from Karen's experiences that there was communication when the two approached death. Here is what Karen had to say:

> During the operation in April, I was aware of an intense feeling of love and compassion. Time didn't exist. I traveled through a kind of tunnel and found myself at a "gate" with three figures. One of them was my grandmother, who was still alive at the time. The other two were unidentifiable humanlike "beings." The feeling of harmony, love, and "goodness" was overwhelming. At one point we were "told" we couldn't pass yet and had to go "back." We were both reluctant.
>
> I went, but my grandmother stayed. The next day my husband told me that my grandmother had

had a stroke and was unconscious and in serious condition. But I already knew.

Then in May, after the doctors saved my life by inserting a drain into my kidney, I woke up after four days. I felt a terrible sadness. It was horrible in the hospital, but when I closed my eyes and dozed off, I could bring back the feeling of love and harmony. Again I had traveled through time and space to this gate. I looked forward to it. My grandmother was still there. We didn't speak words; it was more a "knowing"—communication of a totally different dimension. The light was blindingly beautiful and surrounded everything.

The two "beings" were there again too, and suddenly they let me know it wasn't "my turn" yet. I reached out for my grandmother; her "energy" touched me and became a sort of lacy string of light. She went through, and—still with this tremendous feeling of love—"they" sent me back. When I came around after four days, my family told me my grandmother had died that day. But again, I already knew.[27]

The awareness of Karen's grandmother in both of her shared near-death experiences is remarkable. In Karen's first NDE her grandmother was unconscious from a stroke that would lead to her death a few days later. Both Karen and her grandmother were told that they *"weren't allowed to pass yet and had to go back."* During Karen's second NDE, at the time that her grandmother died, her grandmother was allowed to pass and Karen was not.

This shared NDE shows that heavenly realm encounters with other people or beings are sometimes shared NDEs. Shared NDEs seem to provide a glimpse of the passage into the afterlife of those irreversibly dying and are yet another strong line of evidence for the reality of NDEs and their message of an afterlife.

Skeptics say that near-death experiences can't tell us what happens to those who have permanently departed from this earth. But shared NDEs, while rare, might serve as evidence that what is observed in NDEs is the initial experience of those who have irreversibly died.

CHAPTER 9

Hellish Encounters

Not all unearthly encounters are blissful. The most frightening things that I have encountered in my life were not from fictional books or scary movies, but from near-death experiences with hellish content.

The existence of NDEs with hellish content is puzzling to many. Hellish NDEs are dramatically different from the overwhelming majority of NDEs. They are also completely outside the life experience of nearly all people. However, frightening and even hellish NDEs do exist. They are relatively rare, but still are real NDEs.[1]

One such example of a hellish NDE comes from the NDERF website. I want to include it here so you will have an actual example of how NDErs describe these horrifying experiences.

"Many Souls . . . Weeping and Wailing"

Cathleen C. was given a soft drink laced with strychnine. She realized something was not right when she began to feel distress followed by a loss of hearing, a loss of motor skills, and eventually a dark descent into "hell" that ended in *the deepest, darkest void [she had] ever experienced.*"

Cathleen's experience is unusual since it describes a visit to what she calls "hell" and then her rescue from its torment by angels who then introduce her to what she felt was God. Not only is she permitted to question him about the reason evil exists; she also gets insight into the notion that we all have free will and are allowed to map out our own lives.

Suddenly everything became clear to me. I was dead. I had been created by God. God was a reality, but I wasn't with Him. He was with me, but I didn't know that yet. I began to hear extremely distressing and eventually unbearable noise.

I realized that the noise was countless voices of many souls, saying nothing, only weeping and wailing. It was the most anguished, pathetic sound I have ever heard. The sound of the voices grew and grew until I imagined their numbers were in the millions. It was unbearable; I had to get out of that place. But how? I had no body and no voice. Then deep down in my spirit I screamed as hard as I could. I heard my own voice echoing on and on, "God, help me!" Then

*a gigantic hand came down, moved under me, and
lifted me out of that abyss.*

*I was taken up and up. The anguished voices
faded, and everything was quiet as I realized I was
passing up away from the earth. In moments I arrived at a certain destination and felt confused. I was
concerned about what had happened to my body. I
was facing a group of people I felt I knew, and they
told me not to worry about my body, my former self.
I was with them, and that was all that mattered.*

*They told me I had to talk to a man who was
off in the distance. Then I was immediately in His
presence, and we talked at length. I couldn't hear
His voice, but His thoughts were transferred into my
consciousness and mine into His.*

*I asked Him how I came to be in that place, and
He told me that it was His desire for me to be there
with Him—that he had created me. I told Him that
I hadn't done anything in my life to deserve being in
that beautiful place with Him. He made me understand that He knew everything about me, that I was
who I was because He had created me to be exactly
who I was, and that whatever I was, I was still His
creation, His child, and He loved me so very much.*

*I knew that He had the answers to all questions,
so I asked him, "Why is there evil?" And he replied,
"Because there is good." Then I asked Him, "When
we, your children, come into existence, do we live just
one time, or do we live over and over?" He took me*

to the entrance of a long hall that had millions and millions of doorways leading off of the hall. He made me aware that many choices were available to me, and that that choice was the answer to the question I had asked. The choice was up to me. He made me understand that I could choose to stay with Him or I could choose to walk down the hall and pick a door. He made me aware that picking a door would be my exit out of heaven, and I would be born again out of the womb of a woman on earth. I asked Him, "But how do I know which door to pick?" He replied merely that the door I picked is my choice.

I asked Him, "Do we have to pick another door and live over and over?" That would be hell to me, because what I had experienced in life had largely been sad and distressful. He told me that some people choose to go back, but He doesn't want them to. He wants them to stay with Him, but He understood my feelings. He explained that when we choose to leave Him, He removes all memories of previous lives because He doesn't want us to be distressed. He means for life to be good for all of us. He then reiterated all my choices and again infused me with His love.

He then asked, "Why would you want to leave me?" I don't remember responding. Then He asked, "How do you feel about being dead?" I said that it didn't bother me much; my only regret was that I hadn't been able to say good-bye to my parents.

The next thing I became aware of—amazingly,

remarkably, astoundingly—was that I was in my
body without realizing I had made my choice. I
chose to leave my all-loving, all-accepting heavenly
Father in order to come back and say good-bye
to my parents. My God, what had I given up? I
became depressed beyond words. But here I was
again back in this world. I chose the life I mapped
out for myself.[2]

Cathleen's hellish NDE resembles other NDEs in which the person experiences hell but is then rescued. It is my feeling that this type of NDE may be among the most transformative of all, since it allows a person to see and feel the worst evil and the best good.

A MINORITY REPORT

This section will, out of necessity, be more speculative than any other part of this book. The reason for this is that relatively little research has been done on these types of NDEs, mostly because they are so uncommon. What little research has been done tends to raise more questions than answers.

A 1992 study found three different types of distressing NDEs: (1) typical NDEs that were interpreted by the NDEr as frightening, (2) NDEs with a sense of nonexistence or a frightening void, and (3) NDEs with graphic hellish imagery.[3] An example of the first would be an NDE in which the person uncharacteristically feels fear at being separated from the body at the beginning of the experience. Another example would be an NDE in which elements that are usually seen as positive or neutral—the typical tunnel experience or the presence of angels—are interpreted as ominous or frightening by the experiencer.

In the second type, although encountering a "void" usually feels pleasant or neutral, for some NDErs encountering a void is frightening, because it may be experienced as empty, unconnected, and unpleasant. The third category, hellish NDEs (containing graphic hellish images or occurrences that are of themselves emotionally frightening or distressing), are the least common type of frightening NDEs.

Many near-death experiences are not totally frightening from beginning to end, but have parts that are frightening and parts that are pleasant. When NDEs have both components, it is more common for the frightening part to occur first. The early, distressing stage then eventually transitions into the later, and usually longer, more pleasant stage of the NDE.

Encountering frightening moments during an NDE is unusual, but not rare. The older version of the NDERF survey asked, "During your experience, did you consider the contents of your experience (NOT the possible life-threatening event that led up to the experience) to be wonderful, mixed, or frightening?" The 1122 responses to this question were divided as follows:

Wonderful	722	(64.3 percent)
Mixed	360	(32.1)
Frightening	40	(3.6)

Interestingly, those with frightening NDEs were more likely to indicate they also had a lower level of consciousness and alertness during their NDE than those describing their NDE content as "wonderful." It is intriguing if this could be part of reason their NDEs were frightening.

Hellish NDEs may describe landscapes, entities, or sensations that are unworldly, frightening, and suggestive of classical concepts of hell. Hellish NDEs are a relatively small percentage of all frightening NDEs. It is estimated that about 1 percent of all NDEs shared with NDERF are hellish. Although this is a low percentage, so many NDEs have been shared with NDERF over the years that we have more hellish NDEs available for research than ever before.

Hellish NDEs are difficult to study. It was several years after NDEs were first described in 1975 that the existence of hellish NDEs became more widely known. People tend to interpret hellish NDEs based on their preexisting beliefs, often with a component of fear of negative judgment.

Prior studies of hellish NDEs have established that it is wrong to assume that "good people" have pleasant NDEs and "bad people" have hellish NDEs. In spite of these prior studies, this erroneous stereotype persists. This stereotype may make those experiencing hellish NDEs hesitant to share them.

It is often difficult for near-death experiencers to find the words to describe their pleasant experiences. It is understandable how even more difficult it would be for an NDEr to share an experience that was frightening or even terrifying. NDErs experiencing hellish NDEs are likely aware that they risk negative judgments from others due to the content of their NDEs. Thus those experiencing hellish NDEs may be more comfortable sharing on a website, such as NDERF.

To study hellish NDEs, 26 NDEs containing at least some hellish content that had been shared with NDERF were reviewed. Consistent with the findings of other NDE researchers, our study found a variety of elements in the hellish content, including frightening or threatening beings, hellish landscapes, threatened or actual torture, and communications containing taunts or malevolence. This brief description of the content of hellish NDEs admittedly cannot do justice to the full range of horrific content or depth of emotional terror that is often present.

To help understand frightening and hellish near-death experiences, one important observation needs to be considered. Experiences involving unexpected alterations of consciousness that are not NDEs are much more likely to be frightening than NDEs. These experiences may include intensive-care unit (ICU) psychosis, illicit drug experiences, and so on. It may be reassuring to many individuals who had a frightening experience to discover that their experience was not an NDE.

The great majority of frightening NDEs are not hellish. They are frightening for reasons other than having hellish content. To help understand frightening near-death experiences, some assistance is available from the largest prior study of frightening NDEs, done by Barbara Rommer, M.D. This study reviewed dozens of frightening NDEs.[4] Rommer believed frightening NDEs occur for three reasons: (1) they provide motivation to the NDEr to reconsider prior choices, thoughts, and beliefs; (2) they result from the presence of a less than loving mind-set immediately prior to the NDE; or (3) they result from negative programming during childhood.

From my review of scores of frightening and hellish NDEs on NDERF, I offer my speculation about the cause of frightening NDEs. I am in agreement with the first cause of frightening NDEs suggested by Rommer, but I am less certain about the last two.

Changes in NDErs lives following typical NDEs are generally substantial and quite positively life-changing. These changes following NDEs have been called *aftereffects*. Consistent with the aftereffects of pleasant NDEs, Rommer found that frightening NDEs often result in substantial positive life changes, including a greatly reduced fear of death. Some individuals experiencing a frightening NDE even came to view it as a gift and perhaps the most important experience of their life. As with pleasant NDEs, changes following frightening NDEs may require many years to fully manifest. My review of scores of frightening NDEs leads me to be in substantial agreement with Rommer's conclusions regarding the aftereffects of frightening NDEs.

"I Went Deeper and Deeper into Hell"

One such example of a hellish NDE being a blessing in disguise comes from Frances Z., who wrote her case study for the NDERF website. Frances was a pill addict.

To kill herself she took a hundred narcotic medication capsules with alcohol and lay down to die. Luckily her son came home and found her lying comatose on the floor. Frances picks up the narrative:

> My son ran to the neighbors and told them that something was wrong with me. As they were taking me to the hospital, my heart stopped and from outside of my body I watched them do CPR on me.
>
> As we arrived at the hospital, I began to descend into darkness. I was falling down a very dark tunnel. Demons appeared around me, and even though I was spirit—my body had stayed at the hospital—they were going through the motions of ripping my flesh off. It was intensely painful. As I went deeper and deeper into Hell, I saw many historical figures, and last, my father.
>
> My father welcomed me to Hell, and I thought,

*"This is it for me. My life on earth is over, and I've
ended up in Hell." I didn't think getting out of Hell
would be a possibility, but suddenly I started to go
back up the tunnel toward my body. But I didn't
return completely. I stayed apart from my body and
watched the doctors work on it. As my vital signs
returned, I was pulled toward my body and then into
it. I woke up about ten hours later in the ICU.*

*While I was in the hospital, they suggested I go
to addiction treatment and also recommended that I
address what I had told them had happened to me
when I died. They didn't believe there was a Hell.
But now I've been sober eighteen years and have tried
to help others so that they will never experience the
misery I experienced.*[5]

Frances described her life after her attempted suicide
as one of regaining her zeal for life and adding newly
found compassion. As she put it, *"Before this experience I
did not care about anyone. I was a nurse with no compassion (except when caring for people in hospice). Nowadays I
care very much about my fellow man and try to help whenever possible."*

"You Have to Let Them Know"

And then there's the hellish NDE of the severely alco-
holic John L., who was stabbed in the chest. The knife
was plunged deeply into his upper chest, puncturing his

left lung and slicing through his pulmonary vein.

John's sister pulled him into her car and began driving to the hospital. Although John tried to stay calm, he soon began coughing up blood and *"felt my arms and legs feeling very numb."*

"I'm not going to die," he said to his sister. *"But you'd better hurry up!"*

John inserted the middle finger of his right hand into the wound to stem the bleeding and felt his life slip away. *"So this is it,"* he thought over his sisters screams. Then he passed out.

Here's the rest of the story in John's own words:

I closed my eyes and prepared myself for whatever was coming. My faith had taught me that there would be bright light and peace, so I guess that's what I waited for. Instead, I focused on the little lights you see whenever you close your eyes real hard. They were moving around really fast, but then they began to slow down and disappear, until there was only one left.

I moved through the patterns left by the light, like walking through a cobweb-infested room, but I never felt any sensation of being touched. The sensations increased until I was traveling at incredible speeds. I'm reminded of pictures of astronauts training in a large centrifuge, but I was moving through something—a tunnel, or a tube, or a large open space . . . just moving!

Many voices were coming from different sources,

but the underlying message was to pay attention. They said, "Remember," and "You have to let them know," "You are being shown," and "Don't forget!" I began to think about my life and wondered whether it would be played back and I would be judged accordingly—as my auntie had always told me would happen. And as I was wondering this, I could see all of the things I did throughout my life just as they happened, but faster—the good, the bad, and the ugly. Everything I was proud of and every dirty little secret. I felt remorse, fear, and shame for my indiscretions and understood clearly that we all must account for everything that we do.

I saw thousands and thousands, if not millions, of people moving about aimlessly below me. Each person emitted strong feelings of foreboding, pain, and fear. "These are the lost," a voice told me. Then, as though it was reading my mind, "This is real." I began to feel afraid, but my fear paled compared with what I felt coming from all the people. "What is waiting for me?" I wondered.

I wanted something or someone to hold on to. I could hear childlike laughing and giggling, but it carried an air of seduction. A form came toward me that was neither male nor female, young nor old, living nor dead. I felt like it was mocking me each time it laughed.

This made me angry, but at the same time I was overcome with a strong desire for this being—which had become a seductive and beautiful female. She came closer and pulled me down with tremendous strength and kissed me hard on my neck and shoulder. Again she laughed, and I could feel pain return to my chest.

I looked down and saw blood everywhere! The being was bathed in it! I felt something grab me and say, "Get out of here! What are you doing here?" I was surrounded by people tugging and pulling on me. "Why are you here?" they asked. The woman was suddenly gone, and in her place was a little girl who sat up and smiled at me. But I still felt like I had done something wrong and was in trouble. Was I evil? I frantically looked around for help, but there wasn't any. The people in this hellish place began pushing me away and yelling at me: "Remember to tell them!"

The next thing I heard was, "He's conscious!" and then endless questions, like "What's your name? What's your social security number?" I was alive![6]

Many prior NDE studies used the term "negative" to describe NDEs that were frightening or hellish. I prefer a different label for the hellish NDEs I've studied. Personally, I call them "a walk through the Valley of Death." It is good to remember that most of these are just that, a walk *through* the valley followed by a new earthly life that may be made more positive by these brief glimpses of that place called hell. Also of note is the fact that there is historical literary evidence that past saints and holy men and women have experienced descent into hell. And although this brush with evil may be hard on them, it also often provides the grist for a deeper spirituality, one that moves them to greater spiritual wholeness. That is why I prefer not to think of these hellish NDEs as negative. Rather, they are frightening experiences that can lead to the same level of positive transformation as those NDEs that might be described as pleasant.

HEAVEN AND HELL

As noted earlier, this chapter must be more speculative than the other chapters. It is notable that when NDErs describe hell, it is generally a place fully separated, and distinctly apart, from heaven. An important point is that I never read an NDE describing God casting the NDEr into an irredeemable hellish realm.

My speculation on hellish realms described in NDEs is that beings likely enter hell as a result of very poor choices—likely a great many poor choices. I personally believe that the poor souls in hell have the free will to both make good choices and return to the heavenly realms that seem to be our real homes.

To those questioning what justice there might be for the seemingly irredeemably evil of our earthly existence (such as Adolf Hitler) to have the ability to return to "heavenly realms," I suggest the following: if you believe in our eternal existence, then people acting in profoundly evil ways on earth will have to spend *eternity* fully aware of the malevolent choices they made during their earthly lives. I would expect that God and all other beings around them would also be aware of their evil choices. By my way of thinking, an eternity spent aware of the devastating harm they caused others in their earthly life is a form of hell. Perhaps the evil beings in hell chose to separate themselves from heaven to avoid being known for who they really are.

Hellish realms can be disconcerting to read about. The good news is that throughout this book, you can easily see that the evidence consistently points to a blissful heavenly realm and a God that loves us all profoundly and completely. That is, in my opinion, among the most significant and important messages in the study of NDEs.

CHAPTER 10

God and Religion

Traditional theologians often use the term *omnipotent* to describe God as "all-powerful." Many traditional religious stories emphasize the deity's overwhelming power—whether it is Zeus sending storms or the biblical God destroying Sodom. But in reviewing the near-death experiences that discuss encountering God, we find almost no descriptions of God dramatically demonstrating destructive power. I cannot recall any descriptions in NDEs of God using power to harm any being. This should not be surprising given that in NDEs, God is typically described as profoundly loving. However, descriptions of the power of God are unmistakable when reading near-death experiences:

> ✦ The entire encounter was about God, the ultimate power of God, and God's forgiveness. The message was, "Love is the greatest power in the universe."[1]

◆ I realized I had entered a new dimension of consciousness. I suddenly realized that I was in the control of some being so powerful it was overwhelming. It was the *God* that I tried so hard to believe in on earth.[2]

◆ I became aware of a presence vast and unimaginable, everywhere and everything, the beginning and the end, and he was Love. I came to know that Love is a power to rival all powers—real and perceived—in the universe.[3]

In our earthly lives we may fear what is powerful out of concern that it could harm us. NDErs consistently describe God as powerful but often as powerfully *loving*. In fact, NDErs descriptions of God consistently point to the vital understanding that God is *not* to be feared but rather *embraced*.

THE GOD NDERs ENCOUNTER

This raises the interesting issue of how people's religious ideas affect their near-death experience—and vice versa. If NDEs are merely projections of our ideals and ideas, then how do we explain the discrepancy between some traditional doctrines of heaven and God and the way they are described in NDEs? And how does having an NDE, especially one with an encounter with God, affect these people's expression of religion? These are the questions we will explore in this final chapter.

Near-death experiencers encountering God's insight and wisdom often say that our earthly constructs—such as language, religious doctrine, and others—cannot fully encompass the divine. During their NDEs they may come to understand that our limited earthly vocabulary does not come close to fully describing God. As we have already repeatedly seen, a common lesson from NDErs is that the earthly word *God* might not be the best term for what they encountered.

Natalie was in Iraq in a truck when a huge roadside bomb exploded, severely injuring her. Her NDE was packed with profound spiritual insights including the following:

> *All That Is can be perceived simultaneously as a force and as a consciousness that exists within each individual consciousness and yet is separate from each consciousness or being. It might be called God, but the ideas of gods that we have are a pale and incomplete shadow of the All That Is that I perceived. We project an idea of a god or gods upon that infinite creative consciousness, which inevitably limits our understanding of the All That Is in ways that reflect the limited comprehension that we have of ourselves and the physical universe.*
>
> *The word "God" carries a lot of baggage, and our ideas of "God" are currently deeply inadequate and inaccurate.*[4]

If it is accepted that God is infinite, at least relative to our finite earthly knowledge, then it makes sense that near-death experiencers might balk at using any finite earthly term for the God they encountered. This is consistent with a well-known feature of many NDEs: their experiencers report that what they encountered was often *ineffable*, meaning *incapable of being expressed in words*. It is understandable that if NDEs are often ineffable, then NDErs encountering God may find it especially difficult to describe God in words.

"We All Come from the Same Light"

Regarding the limitations of language when NDErs encounter God, another perspective comes from Maria. She was having a baby when she had a seizure and stopped breathing. Maria shared:

> I wanted to know what to call this light form. It was a pure form of energy. It began to tell me some of the many names for God that our world cultures use. I said that "God" worked for me, even though in my life I didn't know whether I believed in God. I recognized that many of the people I knew would have called it God. We began to communicate. Where was I? Home, familiar place, somewhere I had been many times before. The light wanted to know what I was doing there; I wanted to know too.
>
> I was told that I was too early and still had work to do. What work? I would be able to figure that

out, but I had to go back. I wanted to stay and was immensely sad to have to go. I understood that it was my duty to return and that I wouldn't be asked to do it if I weren't capable. I knew I had to go, but I was afraid. So the light provided me with an escort to guide me safely back.

I'm not afraid of death. Now I know that we are all connected and that each of us is made of light and we are all "God" on earth. I didn't believe in God, and now I accept that we all come from the same light and are part of the light.[5]

The Inadequacy of Language

NDErs typically want to accurately share their remarkable encounters, and earthly language may be inadequate for them. For some NDErs it seems that even all the words in the world's languages cannot accurately describe what they encountered, even if most NDErs choose to call this being "God." The following are the interesting viewpoints of NDErs who encountered what many would call God:

+ "God" is just a small word compared with what I experienced.[6]
+ The Goldenness was all-knowing wisdom, whereas the sheer clarity of the Brilliant Light was what one may call "God." However, it seems to me that we are incorrect to name such Sacred Holiness and power. I can only say that I have witnessed the ultimate of

all that is, was, and ever shall be, yet I can't name that which can't be described.[7]

+ The word we use in this world can't be translated in the world of God.[8]

+ God is everything that can ever be and everything that can never be at the same time, and I'm merely human, so I can understand it only in human terms. Even the best of humanity is still human, so everything will be anthropomorphic. It's like a chair looking at a table and thinking that it sees a strange chair with no back. The chair may never know it is a chair, but it will still function as a chair. It may never question that it is a chair or look beyond its chair-ness, and yet it will be a chair just the same.[9]

+ This presence didn't tell me it was God—that was my later determination—we try to ascribe labels to things that shouldn't have labels. Anyway, this intense energy force wanted to be with me and that was all I cared about at that time.[10]

+ I had the awareness that a spiritual force exists that is all of us combined, not separate. If the word "God" is used, then God is all of us.[11]

"The Spark of the Highest Is in Everything"

One of the most profound near-death experiences ever shared with NDERF came from Amy. She had an allergic reaction to medication. As she hovered near death, she had this NDE:

I always felt that all my actions were being watched "by God" and judged. I believed I often fell short. I didn't have the experience of seeing "God" as an old man in a white robe on a throne, though that's the most prominent image in my mind formerly.

During my NDE, "God" was the Mind, or the "Order" in all things. I felt "God" as the Supreme Highest Vibration and Frequency, which felt like more of an essence than an old man. It was all around me and in everything. And "God" no longer felt male to me—there was no gender. The idea of gender seemed silly because God was all that is beautiful and peaceful and One, and all that is Good.

And everything did feel so good. In fact, I came back with a knowing that despite what seemed "good" or "bad" before, now there was only "Good," because I trusted and knew that everything was in its right place. Even when people made decisions that I didn't agree with, I felt that it was still all "Good."

I also had this knowing that the essence or spark of the Highest is in everything—every mineral, vegetable, animal, and human. I knew that the Highest waited within everything to expand and create and grow and experience. I lost all desire to analyze everything in life, to judge everything as being either "good" or "bad." I wasn't concerned. We are all just consciousness experiencing life and learning how to love, create, and develop to the highest we can be. I

> *now know to choose what feels right, and I do what*
> *I can to work toward harmony when something is*
> *unjust or unbalanced. The universe is full of Order,*
> *so it always finds a way to balance everything because*
> *it can't exist without perfect balance.*[12]

For many NDErs, what they encountered was so different from their prior understanding of God that their questioning of the term *God* is understandable. What we can say is that in NDEs there is a consistent encounter with a loving and compassionate intelligence. What NDErs learn about the nature of this entity is probably more important than what earthly terms they use to describe this entity—whether the term is *God, the One, the Order, Light,* or *Supreme Being.* All these terms point to what I call *God* in this book for lack of a better and widely understood English-language term.

NDEs AND RELIGIOUS IDENTITY

Another insight revealed through these encounters with God in NDEs is about our categories of religion. It is very uncommon that near-death experiencers who encounter God become aware of information about a particular religion. However, some NDErs do. Cynthia was twelve years when she nearly died from a tumor of the pineal gland. As she put it:

*The being was God. I asked Him whether only
people of one religion will make it into heaven. He
said everyone who believes and has faith, even those
who don't think they do, will make it. It depends on
what's in their hearts.*[13]

"Each Religion Is a Pathway"

Jean had toxic shock syndrome so severe that her heart
stopped beating on four separate occasions. She was un-
clear if she met God during her near-death experience,
though she states this about the beings she met in an
unearthly realm: *"The beings in the Temple were definitely
superior to me and filled with such unconditional love too."*
Her NDE had a lot to say about religion:

*I was told that this was the City of God. A man in a
long white linen robe that was tied around the waist
with a cord stood with me at a water fountain. He
said he would take me on a tour and that I could
ask any question I wanted to. Since I had been told
that Catholics couldn't go into other churches without
committing a sin, and that Lutherans thought Catholics were going to hell, I had a very pressing question:
"What is the right religion?"*

*The man told me: "They all are. Each religion
is a pathway trying to reach the same place." I saw
a mountain, and each religious group was trying to
reach the top; they were all trying to get to the same
place. I was then told that people choose to be born*

into whichever religion or group that will help them achieve the lessons they are sent here to learn.

I was told to always look at who benefits with regard to rules that religions make. If it is particular people or the power structure of the religion itself, chances are that the religion isn't of God. Many rules are definitely made by human beings and put into place to benefit either the structure or those in charge.[14]

When near-death experiencers receive information about religion during their NDEs, they generally understand that no earthly religion is the "chosen religion" or the "one true religion." However, God is seldom portrayed as giving NDErs specific instructions about what they should or should not believe in their earthly life. And that includes the religious beliefs of the NDErs.

Religious Self-Categorization

The older version of the NDERF survey asked near-death experiencers to give their religious background at the time of the NDE and also at the time they shared their experiences. For both questions, the three options were "liberal," "moderate," and "conservative/fundamentalist." Of 1,122 NDErs who completed this version of the NDERF survey, there were 144 NDErs who encountered or were aware of God and 978 NDErs who did not encounter God. The religious background of the NDErs at the time of their experiences was:[15]

	NDErs Encountering God	NDErs Not Encountering God
Liberal	47 (32.7 percent)	341 (34.9 percent)
Moderate	56 (38.9)	423 (43.3)
Conservative/ fundamentalist	41 (28.5)	214 (21.9)

Using chi-square statistics, there is no significant difference in religious self-categorization between NDErs who did and NDErs who did not encounter God. This is important because it shows that NDErs who encountered God were not statistically significantly more likely to describe their religious beliefs as "conservative/fundamentalist." If encountering God during NDEs was based solely on preexisting beliefs, it might have been expected that "conservative/fundamentalist" NDErs would have been more likely to encounter God. But that is not what the evidence shows. The evidence is more consistent with the concept that preexisting religious beliefs at the time of the NDEs did not affect the likelihood of their encountering God during their experiences.

The same group of 1,122 near-death experiencers was asked about their religious background at the time that they shared their NDEs, which was an average interval of about twenty years from the time they had their NDEs. The results were:

	NDErs Encountering God	NDErs Not Encountering God
Liberal	60 (41.7%)	405 (41.4%)
Moderate	46 (31.9%)	385 (39.4%)
Conservative/ fundamentalist	38 (26.4%)	188 (19.2%)

Using chi-square statistics, again there was no significant difference in religious self-categorization between NDErs who did and NDErs who did not encounter God at the time they shared their NDEs. NDErs who encounter God are well represented throughout the spectrum of religious beliefs. It seems that encountering God in an NDE is compatible with varied religious beliefs, whether they are liberal, moderate, or conservative/fundamentalist.

The most recent NDERF survey continues to ask about religious background at the time of the NDEs and at the time NDErs shared their experiences. However, it asks about religious background differently than the prior survey. The current survey asks specific details about religious affiliation. There are nineteen possible choices, including options such as "Christian–Protestant," "Christian–Catholic," "Christian–Other Christian," "Unaffiliated–Atheist," "Muslim," "Buddhist," and so on.[16] A review was made of NDErs' religious affiliations. A comparison was made between the religious affiliations of NDErs who did and NDErs who did not encounter God.

The religious backgrounds of NDErs who did and NDErs who did not encounter God were similar. The top four religious affiliations among NDErs who encountered God at the time of their experience made up 74 percent of all affiliations selected in the survey. These affiliations were, in decreasing order of selection by NDErs, Christian–Protestant, Christian–Catholic, Christian–Other Christian, and Other or several faiths. The top four religious affiliations among NDErs who encountered God at the time they shared their experience made up 69 percent of all affiliations selected. They were the same four affiliations as NDErs selected at the time of their experiences, but in a slightly different order. In decreasing order of selection, these affiliations were: Christian–Protestant and Other or several faiths (tie), followed by Christian–Catholic and Christian–Other Christian (tie). This suggests that the most common religious affiliations remain the most common after an NDE that included an encounter with God.

As noted, the most recent NDERF survey continues to ask about religious background at the time of the near-death experiences and at the time NDErs shared their experiences. This allowed an investigation of whether religious affiliation remained the same or changed between the time they had their NDEs and the time they shared them with NDERF. Among the 133 NDErs who encountered God, a slight majority had the same religious affiliation at the time they shared their NDE as they had at the time when their NDE occurred. There were 69 (52 percent) who had the same religious affiliation at both the occurrence time and the sharing time. There were 64 (48 percent) NDErs who had a different affiliation. For the 287 NDErs who did not encounter God, 155 (54 percent) had the same religious affiliation at both the time of occurrence and the time of sharing, and 132 (46 percent) had a different religious affiliation. Thus encountering God during the NDE did not seem correlated with whether the NDErs kept the same or had a different religious affiliation after their NDE.

The NDERF survey questions regarding religious affiliations allowed an optional text response to explain affiliations at the time of the NDE and at the time NDErs shared their experiences. I reviewed the text responses to the religious-affiliation questions for the NDErs who encountered God. The answers by NDErs to the survey question regarding their current religious affiliation were especially revealing. Over and over their comments about their current religious affiliation seemed consistent with what NDErs who encountered God have shared throughout this chapter. What follows are many comments from NDErs who encountered God regarding their current religious affiliation:

+ I didn't feel that the God I met was of a specific religion.[17]

+ I still attend church but now treat attendance as more of a cultural experience than a religious or spiritual experience. Many times I'd like to take over the pulpit and tell people what is really on the other side and that the guilt preached by Christian churches is completely inappropriate.[18]

+ I'm spiritual, not religious.[19]

+ After my NDE I stopped going to church, because I felt that what they were teaching wasn't accurate. I realized that God is pure love and heaven is not somewhere you go when you die; heaven is here now, on earth.[20]

+ I'm not involved in any religion, but I respect everyone and their religion. I no longer look down on people for that aspect of their lives. But I do know that God, in whatever form you choose to believe in him, is real and does exist. But from what I experienced, God is bigger than anything anyone could conceive.[21]

+ No faith now encompasses how I feel regarding life after death or what God is to me. So I have my own faith that comes from within myself. I talk to God, and God talks to me. That is all I need.[22]

+ I attend a nondenominational Christian church. However, I can no longer believe that non-Christians are not accepted in heaven, since during my NDE I was told there was no condemnation and no judgment.[23]

+ The vision and the love that was shown to me have become the whole basis of my belief structure.[24]

+ I'm still very active in my church; however, I'm far more interested in pure truth than in religion.[25]

+ I believe in all walks of faith and belief systems of a higher vibrational loving light power. There is indeed only one "I Am," and this is the power and splendid energy that rules all creation.[26]

+ God is not in a church. He is everything and everywhere.[27]

+ Currently I am a spiritual being with no religious leanings. I know that anything that is not from a place of Love is not of God. My God is loving and compassionate and lives within me as spirit lives in every one of us.[28]

+ I respect the existence of all faiths; all paths merge into one primary goal.[29]

+ I know that God exists, as I have seen God. I am very spiritual but don't attend church. I pray every day throughout the day to God, Jesus, and the Universe. We are all connected.[30]

CHANGES IN RELIGIOUS BELIEFS

These quotes suggest that many NDErs who encountered God underwent significant changes in their religious beliefs after their NDEs. The notion that NDErs' religious beliefs may change significantly after their NDEs is corroborated by the current NDERF survey, which asks, "Have your religious beliefs/spiritual practices changed specifically as a result of your experience?" Of the 133 near-death experiencers who encountered God, the results were as follows:

Yes	97	(73 percent)
Uncertain	7	(5)
No	29	(22)

The responses to this question were compared to those from NDErs who did and NDErs who did not encounter God during their NDEs using chi-square statistics. The NDErs who encountered God were statistically significantly more likely to respond "yes" to the survey question regarding changes in their religious beliefs and spiritual practices. These results suggest that encountering God in an NDE was correlated with a significant change in their religious beliefs and practices.

Another question in the most recent version of the NDERF survey asked near-death experiencers to consider the importance of their religious/spiritual life. NDErs were asked to compare the importance of their religious/spiritual life before their NDE to its importance at the time they shared their NDEs with NDERF. As noted previously, there was an average of about twenty years between the times the NDEs occurred and when they were shared with NDERF. In reviewing the responses to this question from NDErs who encountered God,[31] it was striking how, over time, their belief in the importance of their religious/spiritual life increased:

	Before my experience, my religious/spiritual life was:	At the current time, my religious/spiritual life is:
Greatly important to me	29	110
Moderately important to me	29	12
Slightly important to me	37	4
Not important to me	29	4
Unknown	9	3

It is remarkable how an NDE in which God was encountered was associated with a huge majority of those NDErs to say that their personal religious/spiritual life was of increased importance to them. The responses to this survey question by NDErs who encountered God suggest how profound and long-lasting changes in religious/spiritual beliefs can be. Among the NDErs who did not encounter God, there was a shift toward increased belief in the importance of their religious/spiritual life, but not to the degree seen in NDErs who encountered God. Here are the results for NDErs who did not encounter God:

	Before my experience, my religious/spiritual life was:	At the current time, my religious/spiritual life is:
Greatly important to me	48	187
Moderately important to me	68	54
Slightly important to me	67	16
Not important to me	85	24
Unknown	19	6

There is another point to be made about all this. The substantial changes in these NDErs values and beliefs are entirely consistent with their awareness that their NDEs were *real*. People are unlikely to make large changes in their lives unless there is a good reason. Survey findings like this point to the conclusion that NDErs, both those who did and those who did not encounter God, must have felt that they had a good reason to change toward increasingly embracing their religious/spiritual life. Consistent with everything that NDErs have shared throughout this book, this suggests to me that the NDErs themselves embraced the reality of their NDEs. This also suggests to me that NDErs who encountered God were even more likely to embrace the importance of their religious/spiritual values, because of their awareness from their own personal experiences that *God is real*.

Conclusion

The evidence from the God Study is remarkable. It presents an incredible consistency among NDErs who experience God, heavenly realms, spiritual beings, and other mystical encounters. There is an oft-quoted basic scientific principle that *what is real is consistently observed*. In the God Study, the consistency far outweighs any inconsistency.

In addition to the notable consistency in NDE accounts, there is also an overwhelming majority of NDErs who encountered God and report that their experiences were real. In response to the NDERF survey question, "What do you believe about the reality of your experience at the current time?" 96.2 percent (128 out of 133) of NDErs reported that their "experience was definitely real." This overwhelming majority of NDErs encountering God who believed that their experiences were definitely real is remarkable.

Out of respect for people's ability to generally understand reality, if skeptics want to represent that NDEs are not real, they should present strong evidence that NDEs are not real. Over twenty different "explanations" of near-death experience have been suggested by skeptics over the years. If there were one or even several "explanations" of NDE that were widely accepted as plausible by the skeptics, there would not be so many different "explanations." The existence of so many "explanations" suggests that skeptics have not presented an explanation of NDEs that is accepted by consensus of the skeptics themselves.

Skeptic arguments neither address the consistency of the accounts nor provide hard evidence to disprove their validity. Rather, the God Study provides an opportunity for science and religion to further explore people's experiences of God in NDEs.

It is important to note that near-death experiencers in the God Study come from every walk of life. Among these NDErs are physicians, scientists, nurses, teachers, business executives, homemakers, children, pastors, and others. From these varied backgrounds comes a collection of similar experiences of God and the divine. As a scientist, I find this not only statistically remarkable, but also hopeful. It suggests that life is not random. And the NDErs agree. Here are just a few NDErs' thoughts on their renewed sense of life and meaning after their near-death experience:

◆ All we need on earth is our belief and faith in God and to love, forgive, and accept one another. God loves all creatures.[1]

◆ We can learn and grow, ultimately learning the power we have within us to create our lives if we honor our calling, our divine purpose.[2]

◆ I came to understand that life is an opportunity for us to express and experience love.[3]

These messages of meaning and love can give us hope and direction in our own lives. Even though we struggle to best explain this sense of love and we cannot prove or measure it, we know it is significant and we know it is real. It is just beyond words.

Confounding description even more is the all-inclusive nature of the love these NDE explorers felt. They describe this love as being the very essence of God. Hence, it is the very essence of all reality, the cosmos, life, all things. It is our essence. The light, or energy, behind all creation is or consists of love. That is what NDErs are describing when they talk about the universal love and unity that takes place during their experience, and it is why they often feel as though they have inadequately expressed themselves. Words aren't big enough.

So is that a bad thing? I don't think so. The ineffable is a part of so many big concepts in the universe, and it's the ineffable that drives us on to great discoveries. In fact, it is this quality of these people's accounts that makes them so credible to me. If they are truly encountering a God who transcends our reality, it would sound strange if we heard them say it was all easy to explain or describe. This is why the God Study is an opportunity for us moving forward and further research is encouraged.

Here, in the investigation of the largest collection of near-death experiences to date, we see overwhelming evidence of God. This opens a door for science, for humanity, and for religion. Near-death experiences reveal that death is not an end, but an opening to a wonderful afterlife. I believe this is profoundly good news for all of us.

Notes

CHAPTER 1: **INTRODUCTION**

1. "Source for the Spinoza Quote," ed. Arnold V. Lesikar, *Einstein: Science and Religion*, www.einsteinandreligion.com/spinoza.html.

2. G. Gallup Jr. and W. Proctor, *Adventures in Immortality: A Look Beyond the Threshold of Death* (New York: McGraw-Hill, 1982). The prevalence of NDEs is not known with certainty. The estimate of 5 percent is often quoted in spite of the study's methodological issues.

3. Sam Parnia with Josh Young, *Erasing Death: The Science That Is Rewriting the Boundaries Between Life and Death* (San Francisco: HarperOne, 2013).

4. M. Sabom, "The Near-Death Experience," *Journal of the American Medical Association* 244, no. 1 (1980), 29–30.

5. Raymond Moody, *Life After Life* (Atlanta: Mockingbird, 1975).

6. www.nderf.org/NDERF/NDE_Experiences/gary_nde.htm. Gary NDE 6667.

7. www.nderf.org/NDERF/NDE_Experiences/jeffery_o_nde. htm. Jeffery O NDE 6660.

8. www.nderf.org/NDERF/NDE_Experiences/dharam_s_nde. htm. Dharam S NDE 6645.

9. www.nderf.org/NDERF/NDE_Experiences/corey_l_nde.htm. Corey L NDE 6639.

10. To expand on the inclusion criteria for the NDERF studies quoted throughout the book: The experience had to describe a single NDE and be shared in English on the

English version of the NDERF survey. Second-person NDE accounts were excluded. Further details regarding the survey methodology can be found at http://www.nderf.org/godevidence.

11. The current and prior version of the NDERF survey asks all questions that comprise the NDE Scale. The NDE Scale is described in detail by B. Greyson, "The Near-Death Experience Scale: Construction, Reliability, and Validity," *Journal of Nervous and Mental Disease* 171 (1983), 369–75.

12. There is some variability in what NDE researchers consider the elements of a near-death experience to be. The twelve elements presented here were consistently observed in the NDERF studies.

13. www.nderf.org/NDERF/NDE_Experiences/lauren_nde.htm. Lauren NDE 6774.

14. www.nderf.org/NDERF/NDE_Experiences/dea_m_nde.htm. Dea M NDE 4281.

15. www.nderf.org/NDERF/NDE_Experiences/viola_nde.htm. Viola NDE 6751.

16. www.nderf.org/NDERF/NDE_Experiences/anthony_n_nde. htm. Anthony N NDE 6749.

17. www.nderf.org/NDERF/NDE_Experiences/robert_n_ndes. htm. Robert N NDEs.

18. www.nderf.org/NDERF/NDE_Experiences/irene_nde_6728. htm. Irene NDE 6728.

19. www.nderf.org/NDERF/NDE_Experiences/pamela_k_nde. htm. Pamela K NDE 4649.

20. www.nderf.org/NDERF/NDE_Experiences/melvin_h_nde. htm. Melvin H NDE 3251.

21. www.nderf.org/NDERF/NDE_Experiences/violet_p_nde.htm. Violet P NDE 2969.

22. www.nderf.org/NDERF/NDE_Experiences/richard_r_nde. htm. Richard R NDE 3955.

23. www.nderf.org/NDERF/NDE_Experiences/renee_m_nde. htm. Renee M NDE 2437OBE.

24. www.nderf.org/NDERF/NDE_Experiences/robyn_nde.htm. Robyn NDE 6636.

25. www.nderf.org/NDERF/NDE_Experiences/kathy_k_ nde_6694.htm. Kathy K NDE 6694.

26. www.nderf.org/NDERF/NDE_Experiences/samantha_h_nde. htm. Samantha H NDE 6692.

27. www.nderf.org/NDERF/NDE_Experiences/carol_j_nde.htm. Carol J NDE 5263.

28. www.nderf.org/NDERF/NDE_Experiences/joyce_h's_nde. htm. Joyce H's NDE 2114

29. www.nderf.org/NDERF/NDE_Experiences/inthe.htm. "In the Divine Light,"

30. www.nderf.org/NDERF/NDE_Experiences/robyn_nde.htm. Robyn NDE 6636.

31. www.nderf.org/NDERF/NDE_Experiences/anna_w_nde.htm. Anna W NDE 5426.

32. www.nderf.org/NDERF/NDE_Experiences/judy_h_nde.htm. Judy H NDE 3669.

33. www.nderf.org/NDERF/NDE_Experiences/lillith_nde.htm. Lilith NDE 5376.

34. www.nderf.org/NDERF/NDE_Experiences/kate_b_nde.htm. Kate B NDE 6788.

35. www.nderf.org/NDERF/NDE_Experiences/kristy_c_nde.htm Kristy C's NDE 3745.

CHAPTER 2: THE GOD STUDY

1. See also Mary Jo Rapini, *Is God Pink?: Dying to Heal* (PublishAmerica, 2006).

2. www.nderf.org/Experiences/1timestoodstill.html. When Time Stood Still 3.

3. Further details about updated research findings, a bibliography, frequently asked questions, errata, NDERF study methodology, and a variety of other topics related to the material presented in this book are available on the NDERF website (www.nderf.org/godevidence). The bibliography available there will provide an updated listing of the major sources of information about near-death experience and related topics.

4. For further information about comparing the findings of the God Study with religious beliefs and sacred texts, see www.nderf.org/godevidence.

5. From the same survey of 420 NDErs, 32.4% encountered a tunnel, 25.2% met or were aware of deceased persons and 20.7% had awareness of past events in their lives.

6. Average of 22.3 years, median of 22.0 years, range from 0 to 77.5 years, standard deviation 17.4 years.

7. www.nderf.org/NDERF/NDE_Experiences/cristael_b_nde. htm. Cristael B NDE 6396.

8. www.nderf.org/NDERF/samuel_c_nde.htm. Samuel C NDE 6284.

9. www.nderf.org/NDERF/NDE_Experiences/tonja_bb_nde. htm. Tonja BB NDE 6806.

10. www.nderf.org/NDERF/NDE_Experiences/martin_j_nde. htm. Martin J. NDE 6813.

11. www.nderf.org/NDERF/NDE_Experiences/romy_nde.htm. Romy NDE 7153.

12. www.nderf.org/NDERF/NDE_Experiences/cynthia_y_nde. htm. Cynthia Y NDE 4020.

13. www.nderf.org/NDERF/NDE_Experiences/mary_h_nde.htm. Mary H NDE 6356.

14. www.nderf.org/NDERF/NDE_Experiences/herman_v_nde. htm. Herman V NDE 6227.

15. www.nderf.org/NDERF/NDE_Experiences/rhonda_r_nde. htm. Rhonda R NDE 6343.

16. www.nderf.org/NDERF/NDE_Experiences/arvind_b_nde. htm. Arvind B NDE 6372.

17. www.nderf.org/NDERF/NDE_Experiences/tamara_j_nde. htm. Tamara J NDE 6549.

18. www.nderf.org/NDERF/NDE_Experiences/tyrone_nde.htm. Tyrone NDE 6597.

19. www.nderf.org/NDERF/NDE_Experiences/patricia_b_ nde_6657.htm. Patricia B NDE 6657.

20. www.nderf.org/NDERF/NDE_Experiences/kathy_k_ nde_6694.htm. Kathy K NDE 6694.

21. www.nderf.org/NDERF/NDE_Experiences/tonja_bb_nde. htm. Tonja BB NDE 6806.

22. www.nderf.org/NDERF/NDE_Experiences/tonja_bb_nde. htm. Tonja BB NDE 6806.

23. www.nderf.org/NDERF/NDE_Experiences/joan_lh_nde.htm. Joan LH NDE 6896.

CHAPTER 3: ENCOUNTERS WITH LOVE

1. www.nderf.org/NDERF/NDE_Experiences/julia_o_nde.htm. Julia O NDE 6526.

2. www.nderf.org/NDERF/NDE_Experiences/jeffery_o_nde. htm. Jeffery O NDE 6660.

3. www.nderf.org/NDERF/NDE_Experiences/hannah_nde.htm. Hannah NDE 6665.

4. www.nderf.org/NDERF/NDE_Experiences/anne_n_nde.htm. Anne N NDE 6305/6288.

5. www.nderf.org/NDERF/NDE_Experiences/erinn_h_nde.htm. Erinn H NDE 6155.

6. www.nderf.org/NDERF/NDE_Experiences/paula_s_nde.htm. Paula S NDE 6297.

7. www.nderf.org/NDERF/NDE_Experiences/robyn_f_nde.htm. Robyn F NDE 7209.

8. www.nderf.org/NDERF/NDE_Experiences/john_r_nde.htm. John R NDE 6102.

9. www.nderf.org/NDERF/NDE_Experiences/dw_nde.htm. DW NDE 3587/6106.

10. www.nderf.org/NDERF/NDE_Experiences/camryn_l_nde. htm. Camryn L NDE 6136.

11. www.nderf.org/NDERF/NDE_Experiences/harold_r_nde. htm. Harold R NDE 6141.

12. www.nderf.org/NDERF/NDE_Experiences/erinn_h_nde.htm. Erinn H NDE 6155.

13. www.nderf.org/NDERF/NDE_Experiences/lacy_nde.htm. Lacy NDE 6196.

14. www.nderf.org/NDERF/NDE_Experiences/natalie_s_nde. htm. Natalie S NDE 6246.

15. www.nderf.org/NDERF/NDE_Experiences/rhonda_c_nde. htm. Rhonda C NDE 6138.

16. www.nderf.org/NDERF/NDE_Experiences/mary_h_nde.htm. Mary H NDE 6356.

17. www.nderf.org/NDERF/NDE_Experiences/miles_nde.htm. Miles NDE 6678.

18. www.nderf.org/NDERF/NDE_Experiences/thelma_s_nde. htm. Thelma S NDE 4877.

19. www.nderf.org/NDERF/NDE_Experiences/kathy_w_nde. htm. Kathy W NDE 4416.

20. www.nderf.org/NDERF/NDE_Experiences/bruce_nde.htm. Bruce NDE 5252.

21. www.nderf.org/NDERF/NDE_Experiences/michaele_s_nde. htm. Michaele S NDE 5363.

22. www.nderf.org/NDERF/NDE_Experiences/teri_r_nde.htm. Teri R NDE 4571.

23. www.nderf.org/NDERF/NDE_Experiences/katie_a_nde.htm. Katie A NDE 3183.

24. www.nderf.org/NDERF/NDE_Experiences/demi_b_nde.htm.
Demi B NDE 6405.

CHAPTER 4: UNIVERSAL LOVE

1. www.nderf.org/NDERF/NDE_Experiences/wendy_g_nde.
htm. Wendy G NDE 7373.

2. www.nderf.org/NDERF/NDE_Experiences/veronica_w_nde.
htm. Veronica W NDE 4158.

3. www.nderf.org/NDERF/NDE_Experiences/andrew_p's_nde.
htm. Andy P's NDE 2335.

4. www.nderf.org/NDERF/NDE_Experiences/krikrikit's_nde.
htm. Krikrikit's NDE 2730.

5. www.nderf.org/NDERF/NDE_Experiences/lloyd_p_nde.htm.
Lloyd P's NDE 2764.

6. www.nderf.org/NDERF/NDE_Experiences/anna_a_nde.htm.
Anna A NDE 7433.

7. www.nderf.org/NDERF/NDE_Experiences/leonard_s_
nde_5270.htm. Leonard S NDE 5270.

8. www.nderf.org/NDERF/NDE_Experiences/frank_p_nde.htm.
Frank P NDE 2936.

9. www.nderf.org/NDERF/NDE_Experiences/victor_b_nde.
htm. Victor B NDE 4081.

10. www.nderf.org/NDERF/NDE_Experiences/james_n_nde.htm.
James N NDE 6200.

11. www.nderf.org/NDERF/NDE_Experiences/sheree_f_nde.
htm. Sheree F NDE 6344.

12. www.nderf.org/NDERF/NDE_Experiences/lael_nde.htm. Lael
NDE 6939.

13. www.nderf.org/NDERF/NDE_Experiences/lucia_l_nde.htm.
Lucia L's NDE 2759.

14. www.nderf.org/NDERF/NDE_Experiences/michelle_r_nde.
htm. Michelle R's NDE 2797.

15. www.nderf.org/NDERF/NDE_Experiences/cynthia_y_nde. htm. Cynthia N NDE 4020.

16. www.nderf.org/NDERF/NDE_Experiences/sam_j_nde.htm. Sam J NDE 7352.

17. www.nderf.org/NDERF/NDE_Experiences/raven_r_nde.htm. Raven R NDE 3178.

18. www.nderf.org/NDERF/NDE_Experiences/shannon_t_nde. htm. Shannon T NDE 6119.

19. www.nderf.org/NDERF/NDE_Experiences/bella_j_nde.htm. Bella J NDE 7303.

20. www.nderf.org/NDERF/NDE_Experiences/barbara_s's_nde. htm. Barbara S NDE 7375.

21. www.nderf.org/NDERF/NDE_Experiences/kathy_vb_nde. htm. Kathy VB NDE 7157.

22. www.nderf.org/NDERF/NDE_Experiences/casper_nde.htm. Casper NDE 4210.

23. www.nderf.org/NDERF/NDE_Experiences/peter_k_nde.htm. Peter K NDE 2877.

24. www.nderf.org/NDERF/NDE_Experiences/harold_r_nde. htm. Harold R NDE 6141.

25. www.nderf.org/NDERF/NDE_Experiences/jean_r_nde_6166. htm. Jean R NDE 6166.

26. www.nderf.org/NDERF/NDE_Experiences/michael_h_nde. htm. Michael H NDE 3264.

CHAPTER 5: PURPOSE, MEANING, AND RELATIONSHIPS

1. www.nderf.org/NDERF/NDE_Experiences/john_r_nde.htm. John R NDE 6102.

2. www.nderf.org/NDERF/NDE_Experiences/dw_nde.htm. DW NDE 6106.

3. www.nderf.org/NDERF/NDE_Experiences/ michael_p_nde. htm. Michael P NDE. 6140.

4. www.nderf.org/NDERF/NDE_Experiences/trisha_s_nde.htm. Trisha S NDE 6184.

5. www.nderf.org/NDERF/NDE_Experiences/earl_m_nde.htm. Earl M NDE 6197.

6. www.nderf.org/NDERF/NDE_Experiences/ana_r_nde.htm. Ana R NDE 6118.

7. www.nderf.org/NDERF/NDE_Experiences/shannon_t_nde. htm. Shannon T NDE 6119.

8. www.nderf.org/NDERF/NDE_Experiences/helen_d_nde.htm. Helen D NDE 4507.

9. www.nderf.org/NDERF/NDE_Experiences/demi_b_nde.htm. Demi B NDE 6405.

10. www.nderf.org/NDERF/NDE_Experiences/john_d_ nde_6417.htm. John D NDE 6417.

11. www.nderf.org/NDERF/NDE_Experiences/enocia_j_nde.htm. Enocia J NDE 6291.

12. www.nderf.org/NDERF/NDE_Experiences/kate_d_ nde_6443.htm. Kate E NDE 6443.

13. www.nderf.org/NDERF/NDE_Experiences/bella_f_possible_ nde.htm. Bella F NDE 7660.

14. www.nderf.org/NDERF/NDE_Experiences/lisa_h_nde_5073. htm. Lisa H NDE 5073.

15. www.nderf.org/NDERF/NDE_Experiences/trisha_s_nde.htm. Trisha S NDE 6184.

16. www.nderf.org/NDERF/NDE_Experiences/veronica_m_nde. htm. Veronica M NDE. 6221

17. www.nderf.org/NDERF/NDE_Experiences/marsha_r_nde. htm. Marsha R NDE. 6464.

18. www.nderf.org/NDERF/NDE_Experiences/fergus_j_nde.htm. Fergus J NDE 6524

19. www.nderf.org/NDERF/NDE_Experiences/carol_i_nde.htm. Carol I NDE 5188.

20. The selected exceptional accounts on NDERF are posted at www.nderf.org/NDERF/NDE_Archives/Exceptional%20 Accounts.htm.

21. www.nderf.org/NDERF/NDE_Experiences/jean_r_nde_6166. htm. Jean R NDE 6166.

CHAPTER 6: JUDGMENT

1. www.nderf.org/NDERF/NDE_Experiences/lauren_k_nde. htm. Lauren K NDE 7116.

2. www.nderf.org/NDERF/NDE_Experiences/sharon_b_nde. htm. Sharon B NDE 3670.

3. www.nderf.org/NDERF/NDE_Experiences/casper_nde.htm. Casper NDE 4210.

4. www.nderf.org/NDERF/NDE_Experiences/tamara_j_nde. htm. Tamara J NDE 6549.

5. www.nderf.org/NDERF/NDE_Experiences/barbara_s's_nde. htm. Barbara S NDE 2102/5023/7375.

6. www.nderf.org/NDERF/NDE_Experiences/annette_q_nde. htm. Annette Q NDE 6672.

7. www.nderf.org/NDERF/NDE_Experiences/jenneane_e_nde. htm. Jenneane E NDE 6233.

8. www.nderf.org/NDERF/NDE_Experiences/bruce_nde.htm. Bruce NDE 5252.

9. www.nderf.org/NDERF/NDE_Experiences/florene_w_nde. htm. Florene W NDE 4398.

10. www.nderf.org/NDERF/NDE_Experiences/kim_c's_nde.htm. Kim C's NDE 2669.

11. www.nderf.org/NDERF/NDE_Experiences/elisa_r_nde.htm. Elisa R NDE 4108.

12. www.nderf.org/NDERF/NDE_Experiences/viva_t_nde.htm. Viva T NDE 4397.

13. www.nderf.org/NDERF/NDE_Experiences/stacy_s_nde.htm. Stacy S NDE 4756.

14. www.nderf.org/NDERF/NDE_Experiences/frances_w's_nde. htm. Frances W's NDE 2245.

15. www.nderf.org/NDERF/NDE_Experiences/elisa_r_nde.htm. Elisa R NDE 4108.

16. www.nderf.org/NDERF/NDE_Experiences/erinn_h_nde.htm. Erinn H NDE 6155.

17. www.nderf.org/NDERF/NDE_Experiences/elisa_r_nde.htm. Elisa R NDE 4108.

CHAPTER 7: INSIGHT AND REVELATION

1. www.nderf.org/NDERF/NDE_Experiences/loni_c_nde.htm. Loni C NDE 6861.

2. www.nderf.org/NDERF/NDE_Experiences/barbara_s's_nde. htm. Barbara S's NDE 2102/5023/7375.

3. www.nderf.org/NDERF/NDE_Experiences/charmaine_m_ ndes.htm. Charmaine M NDEs 5313.

4. www.nderf.org/NDERF/NDE_Experiences/melanie_e_nde. htm. Melanie E NDE. 6437.

5. www.nderf.org/NDERF/NDE_Experiences/carol_m_ nde_6496.htm. Carol M NDE 6496.

6. www.nderf.org/NDERF/NDE_Experiences/earl_m_nde.htm. Earl M NDE. 6197.

7. www.nderf.org/NDERF/NDE_Experiences/jean_k_ nde_4964.htm. Jean K NDE 4964.

8. www.nderf.org/NDERF/NDE_Experiences/mike_i_jr_nde. htm. Mike I Jr NDE 4919, 4943.

9. www.nderf.org/NDERF/NDE_Experiences/sandra_h_ nde_4679.htm. Sandra H NDE 4679.

10. www.nderf.org/NDERF/NDE_Experiences/brice_w_nde.htm. Brice W NDE 4906.

11. www.nderf.org/NDERF/NDE_Experiences/jeremiah_j_nde. htm. Jeremiah J NDE 7297.

12. www.nderf.org/NDERF/NDE_Experiences/achild's.htm. A child's NDE.

13. www.nderf.org/NDERF/NDE_Experiences/roland_b_nde. htm. Roland B NDE 6503.

14. www.nderf.org/NDERF/NDE_Experiences/chantal_l_nde. htm. Chantel L NDE 6428.

15. www.nderf.org/NDERF/NDE_Experiences/camryn_l_nde. htm. Camryn L NDE 6136.

16. www.nderf.org/NDERF/NDE_Experiences/cory_g_nde.htm. Cory G NDE 6280.

17. www.nderf.org/NDERF/NDE_Experiences/martin_j_nde. htm. Martin J NDE 6813.

18. www.nderf.org/Experiences/joann_m_nde.html. JoAnn M NDE 638.

19. www.nderf.org/NDERF/NDE_Experiences/jennifer_j_ndes. htm. Jennifer J NDEs 7510.

20. www.nderf.org/NDERF/NDE_Experiences/romy_nde.htm. Romy NDE 7153.

21. www.nderf.org/NDERF/NDE_Experiences/demi_b_nde.htm. Demi B NDE 6405.

22. www.nderf.org/NDERF/NDE_Experiences/martin_j_nde. htm. Martin J NDE 6813.

23. www.nderf.org/NDERF/NDE_Experiences/anne_n_nde.htm. Anne N NDE 6305.

24. www.nderf.org/NDERF/NDE_Experiences/priscilla_o's_nde. htm. Priscilla O's NDE 790.

25. www.nderf.org/NDERF/NDE_Experiences/christopher_j_ nde.htm. Christopher J. NDE 3658.

CHAPTER 8: **HEAVEN**

1. www.nderf.org/NDERF/NDE_Experiences/ellen_k's_nde. htm. Ellen K's NDE 2213/6178.

2. www.nderf.org/NDERF/NDE_Experiences/richard_h_nde. htm. Richard H NDE 3730.

3. www.nderf.org/NDERF/NDE_Experiences/nancy_m_ nde_3825.htm. Nancy M's NDE. 3825.

4. www.nderf.org/NDERF/NDE_Experiences/mary_s's_nde. htm. Mary S's NDE 2190.

5. www.nderf.org/NDERF/NDE_Experiences/brian's_nde.htm. Brian's NDE 2198.

6. www.nderf.org/NDERF/NDE_Experiences/graciela_h's_nde. htm. Graciela H's NDE 2274.

7. www.nderf.org/NDERF/NDE_Experiences/daniel_rs's_nde. htm. Daniel RS's NDE 2364.

8. www.nderf.org/NDERF/NDE_Experiences/janie_g_nde.htm. Janie S NDE 3672.

9. www.nderf.org/NDERF/NDE_Experiences/glauco_s_nde. htm. Glauco S NDE 3674.

10. www.nderf.org/NDERF/NDE_Experiences/paul_t_nde.htm. Paul T NDE 3679.

11. www.nderf.org/NDERF/NDE_Experiences/christopher_j_ nde.htm. Christopher J. NDE 3658.

12. www.nderf.org/NDERF/NDE_Experiences/judy_h_nde.htm. Judy H NDE 3669.

13. www.nderf.org/NDERF/NDE_Experiences/hazeliene_m_nde. htm. Hazeliene M NDE 3725.

14. www.nderf.org/NDERF/NDE_Experiences/shannon_c_nde. htm. Shannon C NDE 6613.

15. www.nderf.org/NDERF/NDE_Experiences/bolette_l_nde. htm. Bolette L NDE 5437.

16. www.nderf.org/NDERF/NDE_Experiences/lavette_h's_nde. htm. Lavette H's BDE 945.

17. www.nderf.org/NDERF/NDE_Experiences/randall_s_nde. htm. Randall S NDE 4955.

18. www.nderf.org/NDERF/NDE_Experiences/claire_b_nde.htm. Claire B NDE 6564.

19. www.nderf.org/NDERF/NDE_Experiences/mike_w_nde.htm. Mike W NDE 122.

20. www.nderf.org/NDERF/NDE_Experiences/erwin_v_nde.htm. Erwin V NDE 5007.

21. www.nderf.org/NDERF/NDE_Experiences/edna_nde.htm. Edna NDE 4965.

22. www.nderf.org/NDERF/NDE_Experiences/nan_a's_nde.htm. Nan A's NDE 720.

23. www.nderf.org/NDERF/NDE_Experiences/kerry_l_nde.htm. Kerry L NDE 3418.

24. www.nderf.org/NDERF/NDE_Experiences/margaret_b_nde. htm. Margaret B NDE 193.

25. www.nderf.org/NDERF/NDE_Experiences/derry_b_nde.htm. Derry B NDE 198.

26. www.nderf.org/NDERF/NDE_Experiences/diane_c_nde.htm. Diane C NDE 321.

27. www.nderf.org/NDERF/NDE_Experiences/karen_vdk_nde. htm. Karen vDK NDEs 6359.

CHAPTER 9: HELLISH ENCOUNTERS

1. See also Nancy Evans Bush, *Dancing Past the Dark: Distressing Near-Death Experiences* (e-book, Nancy Evans Bush, April 9, 2012); http://dancingpastthedark.com.

2. www.nderf.org/NDERF/NDE_Experiences/cathleen_c_nde. htm. Cathleen C NDE 3735.

3. B. Greyson and N. E. Bush, "Distressing Near-Death Experiences," *Psychiatry* 55(1) (February 1992): 95–110.

4. Barbara Rommer, *Blessing in Disguise: Another Side of the Near-Death Experience* (St. Paul, MN: Llewellyn, 2000).

5. www.nderf.org/NDERF/NDE_Experiences/frances_z_nde. htm. Frances D NDE 6242.

6. www.nderf.org/NDERF/NDE_Experiences/john_l's_nde.htm. John L's NDE.

CHAPTER 10: GOD AND RELIGION

1. www.nderf.org/NDERF/NDE_Experiences/robyn_f_nde.htm. Robyn F NDE 7209.

2. www.nderf.org/NDERF/NDE_Experiences/randy_m_ nde_5083.htm. Randy M NDE 5083.

3. www.nderf.org/NDERF/NDE_Experiences/ally_d_nde.htm. Ally D 3019.

4. www.nderf.org/NDERF/NDE_Experiences/natalie_s_nde. htm. Natalie S NDE 6246. This NDEr wrote a book about her experiences in Natalie Sudman's *Application of Impossible Things: A Near-Death Experience in Iraq* (Huntsville, AR: Ozark Mountain, 2012).

5. www.nderf.org/NDERF/NDE_Experiences/maria_s_nde.htm. Maria S NDE 3319.

6. www.nderf.org/NDERF/NDE_Experiences/virginia_d_nde. htm. Virginia D NDE 4591.

7. www.nderf.org/NDERF/NDE_Experiences/yazmine_s_nde. htm. Yazmine S NDE 6992.

8. www.nderf.org/NDERF/NDE_Experiences/mari_l_nde.htm. Mari L NDE 3129.

9. www.nderf.org/NDERF/NDE_Experiences/bridget_f_nde. htm. Bridget F NDE 3648.

10. www.nderf.org/NDERF/NDE_Experiences/elaine_j_nde.htm. Elaine J NDE 4001.

11. www.nderf.org/NDERF/NDE_Experiences/kathryn_h_nde. htm. Kathryn H. NDE 6975.

12. www.nderf.org/NDERF/NDE_Experiencesamy_c_nde_4720. htm. Amy C NDE 4720.

13. www.nderf.org/NDERF/NDE_Experiences/cynthia_h_ nde_5071.htm. Cynthia H NDE 5071.

14. www.nderf.org/NDERF/NDE_Experiences/jean_r_nde_6166. htm. Jean R NDE 6166.

15. For further discussion of the methodology of this part of the study see www.nderf.org/godevidence.

16. For further discussion of the methodology of this part of the study see www.nderf.org/godevidence.

17. www.nderf.org/NDERF/NDE_Experiences/rhonda_c_nde. htm. Rhonda C NDE 6138.

18. www.nderf.org/NDERF/NDE_Experiences/herman_v_nde. htm. Herman V NDE 6227.

19. www.nderf.org/NDERF/NDE_Experiences/natalie_s_nde. htm. Natalie S NDE 6246.

20. www.nderf.org/NDERF/NDE_Experienceswilliam_w_ nde_6292.htm. William E NDE 6292.

21. www.nderf.org/NDERF/NDE_Experiences/mary_h_nde.htm. Mary H NDE 6356.

22. www.nderf.org/NDERF/NDE_Experiences/julia_o_nde.htm. Julia O NDE 6526.

23. www.nderf.org/NDERF/NDE_Experiences/tamara_j_nde. htm. Tamara J NDE 6549.

24. www.nderf.org/NDERF/NDE_Experiences/barry_c_nde.htm. Barry C NDE 6557.

25. www.nderf.org/NDERF/NDE_Experiences/jeffery_o_nde. htm. Jeffery O NDE 6660.

26. www.nderf.org/NDERF/NDE_Experiences/renee_m_nde. htm. Renee M NDE 6683.

27. www.nderf.org/NDERF/NDE_Experiences/loni_c_nde.htm. Loni C NDE 6861.

28. www.nderf.org/NDERF/NDE_Experiences/karin_f_nde.htm. Karin F NDE 7291.

29. www.nderf.org/NDERF/NDE_Experiences/maggie_s_nde. htm. Maggie D NDE 7361.

30. www.nderf.org/NDERF/NDE_Experiences/wendy_g_nde. htm. Wendy G NDE 7373.

31. For further discussion of the methodology of this part of the study see www.nderf.org/godevidence.

CONCLUSION

1. www.nderf.org/NDERF/NDE_Experiences/shannon_t_nde. htm. Shannon T NDE 6119.

2. www.nderf.org/NDERF/NDE_Experiences/steve_l_nde.htm. Steve L NDE 6244.

3. www.nderf.org/NDERF/NDE_Experiences/enocia_j_nde.htm. Enocia J NDE. 6291.